The Copy Code

How To Write *Irresistible* Advertorials…

That Turn Ice Cold Prospects Into Cold Hard Cash

By: Tiffany Alford

Table of Contents

Intro: 8
Section One: The fundamentals of copywriting 12
Chapter 1 - What is Copywriting? 13
Chapter 2 - What is the purpose of copy? 16
Chapter 3 - 12 Key Elements To Successful Copy 20
Section Two: Warming Up Your Audience 24
Chapter 4 - "Ice Cold" To Summer Warmth 25
Chapter 5 - 4 Step Funnel Guaranteed To See Results 30
Chapter 7 – Opt-in Page Strategies 40
Section 3: How to be different 44
Chapter 8 – How To Capture The Eye Of Your Reader 45
Chapter 9 - Writing A *Captivating* Headline 52
Chapter 10 – Create a compelling sub-head 76
Chapter 11 – Stand OUT with a Banner 78
Section 4: How to write a story 82
Chapter 13 – Where to begin? 88
50 POWER WORDS YOU CAN USE TO INCREASE THE PULL OF YOUR COPY: 113
Section 6: Know your audience 115

Chapter 15 – Who does your audience hate?....... 117

Chapter 16 - Are you on their side? 120

Section 7: The turning point 123

Chapter 17 - The AHA! Moment............................ 125

Section 8: What can you do for them? 129

Chapter 18 - How can you benefit them?............. 130

Section 9: Credibility 133

Chapter 19 – Give PROOF 134

Chapter 20 - Why you need a group..................... 139

Chapter 21 - Get more page likes.......................... 141

Chapter 22 – Testimonials sell themselves........... 143

Section 10: What do you have to offer? 145

Chapter 23 - Introduce your offer (pitch) 146

Section 11: Give more than you get 149

Section 12: What is it worth?................................. 155

Section 13: Secondary content 161

Chapter 26 - How can you use a sidebar?............. 163

Chapter 27 - Link to a blog site 167

Chapter 29 - Promote affiliate products............... 171

Chapter 30 - CTAs (Call To Actions) 176

Chapter 31 – Lead generating CTAs....................... 179

Section 15: Push them over the edge.................... 185

Chapter 32 - Persuade them with scarcity 186

Section 16: How can you reassure them? 189

Section 17: How should it all look? 195

Chapter 34 - Advertorial samples 196

~ SAMPLE 2 ~ 201

~ SAMPLE 3 ~ 207

~ SAMPLE 4 ~ 213

~ SAMPLE 5 ~ 217

~ SAMPLE 6 ~ 225

~ SAMPLE 7 ~ 231

~ SAMPLE 8 ~ 237

Section 18: What's next? 239

Chapter 35 - Email marketing 240

Chapter 36 - Lead Magnet delivery 245

Chapter 37- Abandoned Cart Emails 249

Chapter 38 - Promo Emails 253

~ Email Sequence 1 ~ 255

~ Email Sequence 2 ~ 261

~ Email Sequence 3 ~ 276

~ Email Sequence 4 ~ 287

~ Email Sequence 5 ~ 299

~ Email Sequence 6 ~ 329

CONCLUSION: 343

Glossary: Marketing Terms to Improve Your Marketing Vocabulary 345

Intro:

1 What is this book about?

So, you want to start an online business...and would like to know where to begin?

Well, you've come to the right place.

The Copy Code will walk you through what you need to start generating leads,
The Copy Code will show you the importance of copywriting,
The Copy Code will deliver valuable techniques you can use to write successful advertorials

Once I've shown you how to write a compelling advertorial, I'm going to show you what a successful one looks like.

You see, I'm literally leaving you with 8 advertorial samples in this book, to give you inspiration for your future ones.

Plus, I'm including my email swipes for over 40 emails you can use them as insight to help you write irresistible emails that make your subscribers TAKE ACTION!

You'll want to give this book your FULL attention and take notes when you find a golden nugget you can use right away (I'm confident there will be plenty of them for you!).

2 Who is this book for?

Let's be frank, this book isn't for everyone.

Are you looking to generate more leads for your business?

Do you want to understand the fundamentals of copywriting to increase your conversions?

Will you take action, if I show you exactly what to do and how to get results?

If you've answered "Yes!" to any of these questions, then this book was written specifically for you.

If you've answered "No!" then this may not be up your alley, and you may want to check out another book.

You see, I only want to show this valuable information to those who are seeking answers when it comes to improving their business and increasing their subscribers.

If you're not going to take what I show you and put it into action for your own business, then it would be a waste for you to read this book.

However, I'm confident, you're not this type of person.

In fact, since you're still reading, I can safely assume you're ready to make a change and start seeing some massive results with your business.

Am I right?

If I am, then continue reading because I'm about to revolutionize the way you see "lead generation" and make it easier than you ever thought possible!

Section One: The fundamentals of copywriting

Let's jump right in. It's only logical, we begin with Copywriting.

So, this section will break down the fundamentals of Copywriting, show you what it takes to write successful copy, and explain why it's so important if you want to see massive results!

Take your time, highlight certain key nuggets that stand out to you and I hope this helps you make massive conversions.

Chapter 1 - What is Copywriting?

Copywriting? Isn't that the little ™ at the end of the logo or product name?

This is the commonly asked question and the biggest misconception about copywriting.

In fact, if you own a business, have a website or market a product/service in any way, you've probably used copy in some way or another.

Copy can be used in emails, landing pages, newspapers, blogs, flyers, brochures, you name it.

It's literally "salesmanship" in print!

You see, you can have an AMAZING product, but if your copy doesn't speak to your audience or resonate with their current life, then they won't buy from you, and you'll lose their interest completely.

Frankly, copywriting is the fundamental key to transitioning a cold prospect into a loyal customer.

Unfortunately, this also means if you have a terrible product but GREAT copy, you'll probably still sell a good portion of it.

The thing is, you won't have any *returning* customers if your product is terrible and doesn't deliver or solve the problem as promised.

You'll basically get a bunch of one-time sales, and this is no way to scale up a business.

But if your product solves a problem, helps change their life in a good way and delivers what you promise - plus your copy is on point - you'll have an endless supply of customers returning for more and always excited for your next product.

And if you give this book your full attention, I'll walk you through the aspects of copywriting, what it takes to convert your audience using words, plus how to build a bond with your audience using your copy.

It's not hard once you understand the fundamentals, you'll have infinite opportunities to use your skills and make some massive results happen!

This next chapter will take you through the purpose of copywriting and how it can make such a HUGE difference for you.

Chapter 2 - What is the purpose of copy?

Some marketers have been skeptical about copywriting and what it can do for their business.

Questioning whether it's important if it can make a difference and whether or not they should actually be using it.

Well, if you want your audience to like what you have to say, then you'll need to determine what it takes to resonate with them.

This takes some time and a little training in the art of copywriting.

You see, your audience could click on your ad just because they like your picture.

But once they get your website and your copy is downright terrible, they lose interest.

If it's choppy, too intelligent for them, too long, or even too sales-y ... you could lose their interest and lose the sale (or lead).

The whole purpose of your copy is to:

(1) Grab Attention,
(2) Entice Them To Continue Reading

(3) And Encourage Action

You can't do this, unless…you include benefits, write a story, and be personal versus straight pitching your audience.

You may be asking yourself, "why should I care about my content this much?"

There's simple answer to this.

You can have visitors to your website who click off immediately, or you can have visitors who engage with your site and take action towards what you're offering.

Think about it…

The last time you visited a website where you were instantly turned off by the headline or the story didn't catch your attention, and you went back to google to search again.

The headline could look too sales-y, the content could be boring, the facts could sound like a bunch of bull, or the layout could be confusing to look at and hard to read.

There's plenty of reasons for someone to click the back arrow or exit out of the window altogether.

This is why you'll need to take the time to think your content through and ensure your copy speaks directly to your audience without repelling them away from your website.

The easiest way to do this is with a story, delivering value and showing possible solutions.

You'll want to capture their attention, without them noticing the fact you're taking up their time.

They need to be so engulfed in your story, it's like they have stepped into your world and the world around them no longer exists.

You have their FULL attention, and nothing could distract them.

Your only mistake could be losing their interest when the world around them becomes more fascinating than you.

Make your story adventurous, action packed, and emotional enough to keep your audience hanging on until the very last second.

Walk them through the pain they've experienced, the life they could have been experiencing and the dreams they've put on hold.

Then once you have them right where you want them, ready to take action and hanging on your every word…BAM!

You hit them with an offer or possible solution.

Give them an answer to all of their problems, the key to living life the way they want to.

This could mean, you're giving them the best skin care solution, or a master course on webinars, or even access to a monthly membership where they get coffee mugs delivered to their door.

It doesn't matter what you're selling – the BEST way to get your point across is with a story, leading into how you can save the day with your product/service.

But let's be frank, if your product doesn't deliver or solve the problems as promised, you won't have any *returning* customers.

And you may have a HIGH return rate as well.

I'm pretty confident your product/service is AMAZING and will deliver some incredible results for your customers.

So, don't forget to give your copywriting an extra boost, it could be the difference between getting a ton of visitors with no sales and generating a massive list of leads who want to buy from you!

Chapter 3 - 12 Key Elements To Successful Copy

Each element of copywriting plays into each other, and with the perfect balance your copy will have your audience on the edge of their seats desperate to see what you're going to say or offer next.

Here are the 12 major elements of successful copy:

1. **Headline -** The very FIRST thing your audience will read... it's SUPER important!

2. **Sub-headline -** This sentence will lead them into the opener and determine if they keep reading...

3. Opening - This needs to hook them in with a story, making them settle into their seats waiting to see what else you'll say

4. Pain Points - Walk your audience through the suffering they're currently experiencing, this helps identify the problem they're having

5. AHA! Moment - The plot twist, where you had an epiphany about a solution…

6. Possible Solution - Introducing your product/service and how it's helped others…

7. Benefits! - Don't forget to show them how it will change their lives, how it will improve them and solve their problems

8. Social Proof - This is where you can include testimonials, reviews, case studies and any other proof you can use to show them it works!

9. Your Pitch - Offer your product/service as the best option and easier solution

10. Guarantee - They want to feel like this is a risk-free investment, and they'll see the results they want from it - here's your chance to reassure them

11. Scarcity - Here's where you can make them feel like, they may be left behind if they don't take action right away…

12. Call To Action - Now your prospect is interested and wants to buy…so you need to tell them exactly what to do to get access to your product/service

Now that you know what the key elements are, I'm going to be diving deeper into each one to ensure you completely understand the purpose and how to create them yourself.

I want to make sure you're 100% confident in your writing skills, to be able to write an advertorial any time you need it and generate leads/sales from it almost immediately. Sometimes you can leave out one section or another, and your copy will still convert.

It's all about which stage in the sales process you're at, where this copy is going and what the purpose is.

For your advertorial, you want to use every one of them.

Don't know where to start?

Don't worry, I'll show you every step in detail and walk you through what needs to be said to attract an audience.

Stay tuned and give your full attention to this next section.

Section Two: Warming Up Your Audience

Now, you know why copywriting is essential to a successful business.

This next section will walk you through:

- ✓ **Using Words To Capture Attention & Deliver Value** – making your copy, irresistible to your audience

- ✓ **What To Say To Convert Your Audience** - from a cold prospect into a warmed up "lead"

- ✓ **5 Small Tweaks To Ensure Better Conversions On Your Website** – it only takes a 1% increase to see a huge difference, imagine having a 5% increase…

You'll be amazed at what you can do with just the right amount of copy and the perfect balance of value.

Don't look now, but you're about to see what most of our sales funnel look like, and how we've managed to convert Facebook traffic into leads.

This is packed with techniques and strategies you can use right away to see a difference.

Take advantage of what I'm about to show you and put it into action for your own business.

Let's jump right in, I'll see you on the other side.

Chapter 4 - "Ice Cold" To Summer Warmth

Your target is someone who doesn't know you...what do you do?

The rule of thumb is for your audience to:

Know You, Like You, Trust You To Buy From You

So, the first step is bringing awareness to your audience, introducing yourself and your business.

At this point, your audience is a COLD audience, one who has no clue who you are or why they should listen to you.

Ok, so your prospect is looking to "save" their own life, right now.

They've been searching hours, days and even weeks for the solution.

It just so happens that your product is exactly what they are looking for.

Except when they reached your website, they didn't feel a connection and couldn't understand fully, what you're giving them.

It's a common mistake, and easy to fix.

The most common technique is by "showing" and not "telling" them what you can do them.

Using emotions and stories can increase your conversions, easily.

All you need to do is change your professional dialogue to a more conversational one and change your words from "rational" to "emotional."

For example, instead of saying "Concerned" you can say "worried" and instead of saying "immediately," say "Right now."

Lately there has been a flood of people asking about "Website Content" and how to get better conversion rates.

To help out, I'm going to reveal 5 ways to boost conversions without using a Copywriter. :D

Before I reveal this, I want to say thank you for your feedback and questions, it keeps me on my toes :)

Booster #1: Make sure to address your client's more important objections right up front and why they should stay on your website

Booster #2: Sometimes, your reviews will sell better than you do. So, include an option to read and leave reviews, plus offer a coupon for doing this

Booster #3: If your audience is visiting your website for a promotion or coupon, automatically fill in the coupon at checkout if possible

Booster #4: Avoid "mental blockers" by keeping your ad and your landing page in the same color scheme and corresponding copy

Booster #5: Be more personal with your audience. Create comfort and familiarity by personalizing the landing page to include what they searched for and where they came from to visit your site

For example, include "Attention: Network Marketers" when they're searching for network marketing tools.

Make sense?

Here are two quick tips for website conversions:

Tip #1: Make your content easier to read by cutting the paragraphs short after 4 sentences

Tip #2: Make sure your website loads fast, or your audience will click away even faster.

Frankly, the average attention span is too short to consider staying on your website after a slow load.

Just one small edit can change your whole conversions...

...continue tweaking it until it's performing the way you want it to.

Chapter 5 - 4 Step Funnel Guaranteed To See Results

The best part about marketing these days is the blessing of having Facebook.

No matter who your audience is, you can find them on Facebook, from ages 18 to 90 years old.

You see, Facebook does ALL the work for you.

They've collected data on just about everyone, worldwide.

They know what books your audience is reading, what movies they hate, what they like to buy and what events they go to.

They even track down what the stores they buy from, putting ads from those stores right in front of them.

Lucky for us, we can tap into this data Facebook has collected and targeted a specific person for our products/services.

However, Facebook likes to make it tricky sometimes.

In fact, they've recently changed their rules, and have different regulations for your opt-in pages or any website your Facebook ad is linked to.

You see, they want to make sure you're not a SCAM or a robot, looking to steal from people and cause mischief wherever they go.

The best way to avoid being labeled SCAM is by linking to your Facebook ad with an advertorial.

This way your ad catches their attention, your advertorial informs them and warms them up then your sales page closes them.

It's the perfect sales process.

Taking a cold lead, warming them up and building a connection before trying to sell them on anything.

You're more likely to convert your prospects if you're not hounding them or demanding they buy.

Look at this way, you're breaking down their skepticism, disputing their excuses and showing them you have a possible solution.

They can take it or leave it.
But it makes it seem like it's more their choice, instead of being pushed into something they don't want.

How do you write a successful advertorial?

Writing Profitable Advertorials Is A "Piece Of Cake" When You Use This Simple 4 Step Strategy...

I'll let you in on a secret.

The fastest way to promote your business, the easiest way to create compelling content and the best-looking format to do it ALL... **is with an Advertorial.**

You may have heard about it but what commonly gets misinterpreted is, **Advertorials are ALL about being subtle** and selling the audience with more content than pitch.

They are literally **an advertisement hidden inside an article** of content, giving your audience the illusion of NOT being sold.

Let's face it, most people LOVE buying objects and materials, **but they HATE being sold anything**.

So, here's are 5 steps you can follow to easily write a profitable advertorial with just the right amount of pitch and exactly the right amount of content that your audience is looking for.

Step #1: Your headline MUST create urgency, curiosity and trigger a pain point ALL at once

You see, your headline does MOST of the work for your copy. It's literally the first thing your visitors will see. This means, if your headline doesn't strike your audience and grab their complete attention, then they'll click away faster than you can say, "Hold On, Let Me Show You This Before You Leave!"

Your headline has 3 seconds to gain their attention and trigger them to take action by continuing to read on.

Step #2: Write in the voice, your audience will understand

You want your advertorial to resonate with your audience from the beginning. This means writing in their voice and continuing the story that's already playing out in their mind.

The easiest way to do this is, by using websites that sell books in the same niche/industry as yourself.

After reading through their reviews (good & bad), you'll be able to pick up their tone of voice, pain points and what they like about your type of products.

Tip: Remember to look at the bad reviews too, the negative outlook gives a better perspective about your audience's pain points... Which is exactly what you want to trigger!

Step #3: A sales pitch in disguise…

Again, people do NOT like being sold, they'll go out of their way to avoid salespeople!

With this in mind, your content must not look sales-y or to corporate looking. You can even use some of the news websites and popular blogs to pinpoint the look that's working with your audience right now. It helps to ensure your readers can easily scan and follow along with your copy.

This means, breaking up large sections and creating **BOLD** sub-headlines to help keep the readers' eyes comfortable. But remember, you want to give more value than you take. So, keep any sales talk until the very end, where you subtly ask for them to take action.

Step #4: Ask for their attention and feedback

To better understand your audience, ask for their feedback with comments below your advertorial. This will also help send the message that you're real, making people like and trust you.

Once they like it, ask them to share it with their friends. The more people know about you, the more people will like you. And as the saying goes, "If they know you, like you, and trust you…they'll over and over again."

<u>Now you know the main steps to creating your advertorial…let's break it down a little more.</u>

You see, there's plenty more that goes into writing an advertorial which will actually, convert your audience and produce results for you.

But rest assured, you're about to see it ALL.

I'm going to tell you EVERYTHING I know about advertorials and how to use them to expand your business even past your own personal goals!

Chapter 6 – Advertorial vs. An Article

Think about the last time you read an article.

When you were reading it, did you feel like you were being sold something?

Or did you feel like you were learning something new?

The thing about an article is, it's solely meant to inform your audience, give them some valuable tips and maybe even, deliver a "freebie" (but more on that later).

However, when you're using an Advertorial, your main goal is to warm up your audience for a sale.

In fact, an advertorial consists of half "article" and half "advertisement" to form the perfect blend of both.

Here's the skeleton of a GREAT article:

- ✓ Headline
- ✓ Story/Value
- ✓ Bullet
- ✓ Bullet
- ✓ Bullet
- ✓ Conclusion/Call To Action

An article is meant to deliver value, and introduce your audience to something new…something they've never seen or heard of before.

You see, your audience has landed on your article for one of two reasons, you have the answers they were looking for or you have something they want to learn about.

Either way, you have their full attention and they expect you to deliver some amazing news.

This is very similar with an advertorial.

In fact, you'll want your advertorial to do the exact same thing.

You want it to pull your audience in with the promise of more information on a topic they're currently interested in.

But you also want to come at them from a "friendly" point of view.

Let me explain.
The reason articles work so well, is because you know when you're reading an article it's written by a *person*.

Someone you can see as an average joe, breaking down something nobody else could explain to you.

It's like they knew exactly what to say to make sense to you.

And you instantly felt a connection with them.

Like, if they could something like this and instantly understand, then you can too!

This thought process leaves you feeling like you must read the article and understand what they're saying, and try it out for yourself.

You're not trying to buy something.

You're not talking to a salesperson.

You're talking to someone who has been there, done that and is successful because of it.

If this is what you want in life, then you'll definitely read the article and figure out how to do it yourself, right?

Well, this is the way you want your audience to feel.

This is the "article" element you want to include in your advertorial.

You definitely DON'T want to come off as a sales page.

You don't want to come off as a sales person.

And you definitely don't want to push your audience AWAY.

You want to attract them and convert them, in the easiest way possible.

Chapter 7 – Opt-in Page Strategies

"Don't over think it.

Just sit down, come up with a headline and ask for their contact info.

It's not that hard."

WRONG!

It may not be hard, but it's definitely not something you want to brush off as not important.

You see, when it comes to your landing page, you need to convert your audience or there's no purpose to it.

In order to convert your audience, you would need an incentive, something they will get in return for giving you their information.

Once you have your incentive, it's all about presenting it in an attractive way.

You want them to want it SO bad, they won't think twice about giving you their info for it.

The best way to do this is to NOT sell the incentive but to show them what the incentive can do for them.

In other words, show them the BENEFITS.

For example, if you're using an eBook as your incentive then you'll want to include a small line saying something like,

"Get Your FREE Book Right Now!" or "Download Yours FREE Today!"

This type of line will go above your headline and draw attention to your copy.

Now, you have their attention, you'll need to use the headline to drive them to want your book.

Saying something like,

"Get Access To Our New Book, Where We Break Down _____ & Show You Exactly What To Do To _____."

This is straight to the point and pretty short, but you can add to it.

After you've written your headline, next comes your sub-headline.
Here's where you can include a call to action to direct your audience to click the button or fill out the forms for you.

For example, "To get instant access to your eBook, fill out the form below and click the button to be taken directly to it – enjoy..."

The button is where most people will go wrong.

You see, you'll want the button to speak for the prospect not TO the prospect.

Let me explain.

When you're talking 'to' the prospect, your button would say,

"Download Right Now!" or "Order Yours Here!"

Instead, let the button speak FOR them.

I.e., "Yes! I Want This NOW!" or "Yes! I Want Access To _____!"

See the difference?

On one side, you're demanding action.

On the other side, your audience is identifying with your button and admitting they want what you're offering.

These tend to convert better and have been seeing incredible results.

Also, here are 3 tips for making sure your landing page is a HUGE success:

1. Don't clutter your page – keep it short and to the point, with a picture your headline, sub-headline, and button (you can add a couple more lines, but too much will repel your audience rather than attract them).
2. Your picture needs to be relevant – however, it needs to stand out as well…so, if you're doing something for family, include a "happy" family picture in the background – if it's for summertime, include a group in their bathing suits, etc.)
3. Make sure you're using the BIGGEST pain point or benefit – you want to use the pain point or benefit which will trigger the biggest emotional response and encourages them to take action fast!

Section 3: How to be different

You have three seconds to catch my attention...QUICK, what will you do?

This is the same concept you need to keep in mind for your landing pages, your ads, and any type of copy you use.

If you can't capture their attention, then your ad won't be clicked on and your sales page will be ignored.

Frankly, this is the fastest way to lose your audience and sink into debt rather than making sales like you want/need to be doing.

The best part is, I'm about to show you exactly how you can capture attention, give you helpful techniques to use right away and even reveal the importance of a sub-headline.

Some of this may sound familiar; however, I'm going to revealing a ton of things I haven't shared with anyone else.

Turn the page and see what's in store for you...

Chapter 8 – How To Capture The Eye Of Your Reader

The key to capturing attention is by standing out from the crowd!

Your content needs to POP! and grab their attention before they dismiss you altogether.

Imagine a stampede of bulls, if you look like another bull, you won't be noticed.

But, if you look like a horse, you'll be spotted right off the bat.

It's all about standing out and being different, even if it's in the slightest way.

Sometimes it can be a color that stands out the most, like red when everyone else is using blue.

Or it can be the background of your website, or the picture you use.

There are endless ways to make your website look different. (more on that later…)

An uncommonly known way to capture attention is by resonating with your audience.

It's not just about standing out.

Just by standing out and looking "different," you can catch their attention for a mere 3 seconds.

However, to convert an audience, you need more of their time and their complete attention.

These days, distractions are everywhere.

Your readers could be at school, sitting in their office at work, checking their email right quick, or just taking the time to explore the web.

No matter what they're doing, there's always something within reaching distance that could steal their attention away, and then you've lost them forever.

To ensure this doesn't happen, you can stand out, but you also need to resonate with them.

A better way of saying "resonate" is to make your copy seem "familiar" to your readers.

How can something they're seeing for the first time seem familiar?

Simple, you can revolve your whole story and copy around your audience's life.

If they feel like you're talking about "them" specifically, and you've struck a chord with them, then they will think you've written your advertorial solely for THEM.

See where I'm going with this?

Your audience wants to feel special or feel like you're their friend, not someone who is trying to sell them on something.

But you also need them to know, you're steps ahead of them.

You've been where they're at, or you've witnessed a friend go through the same situations.

You know what problems they're going through, and you know how to help them solve those terrible problems.

If they feel like you have the answers, then you have their attention until you give them those answers.

Once you have their attention, you can lead them on with more valuable information, answers to other questions, and sell them on multiple products.

In fact, if you're always delivering valuable information and solving their problems, you'll have loyal customers for life.

Remember, to sound "familiar" you'll want to make it look like you're speaking directly about their life.

Helpful tips for capturing attention and resonating with your audience:

- ✓ Use bright colors to capture the eye – colors like orange, red, yellow, and even blue have been seeing some great results
- ✓ Do NOT confuse the eye with crazy color schemes – black words on white background works great, don't get too fancy with the black backgrounds and colorful words…it confuses your reader and makes it even harder to read
- ✓ Use emotional questions as headlines and sub headlines – you want them to feel sad, depressed, excited, angry, curious… pick an emotion and create a question which triggers this specific emotion, it helps "trap" them in for more reading
- ✓ Use stickers and badges – you can use an arrow to point to where you want them to start reading or use a badge to establish your page as an authority figure in the industry
- ✓ Use banners to call attention to the top of your page – they could include a question,

a call to action, a hyperlink or just tell them to continue reading...

Keep in mind, you want your content to be "attractive," not a repellant.

So, here are 9 different types of attractive content we all desire to read:

1. "Journey" Content – where we're taken on an adventure with a story
2. "Matter" Content – where we're reminded we matter in this world
3. "Revealing" Content – where we're get exclusive access to uncommonly known secrets
4. "Twisted" Content – ones with unexpected twists throughout the entire story
5. "Challenging" Content – where our assumptions are challenged
6. "Edu-Taining" Content – where we are educated while being entertained
7. "Dream" Content – where we're reminded our dreams can come true
8. "Fresh" Content – where we are given a fresh look at something even if it's a common thing
9. "Tearful" Content – where we're brought to tears whether it's from crying or tears of joy

The next couple chapters will walk you through writing an irresistible headline and following it up with a juicy sub headline.

You'll definitely want to take your time and give it your full attention!

Chapter 9 - Writing A *Captivating* Headline

Your headline is the very FIRST thing your audience will see. (if you don't have a banner above it...)

You have 5 seconds to intrigue them and show them you have something they would love to have.

Here are the 4 "U's" for writing an irresistible headline:

1. Make sure your headline is UNIQUE (you can swipe a headline, but give it your own touches – don't just copy, word for word)
2. You'll want to keep your headline ULTRA specific (don't be subtle, get to the point and show them you have the answers)
3. Your headline should spark some URGENCY in your readers (you want them to take action right away, giving you their attention and to continue reading what you have to say...)
4. Oh, and don't forget to make your headline USEFUL (you want it to be relevant to your audience's life at this moment, to catch their eye like "current news" or breaking news)

You see, your headline is doing all the HEAVY work for you and your copy.

This means, if your headline doesn't catch your audience's eye, then there's no use in writing any further because they won't read it.

Before you freak out, here are over 200 headline templates you can use (just input your information and make it your own):

1. **How you can transform your life with <benefit>**

2. **How you can turn your life 180 degree with <benefit>**

3. **'<#> free <benefit> that allow you to <goal>**

4. **How to <goal> effortlessly**

5. **How to <goal> and <benefit> in <timeframe> effortlessly**

6. **Master the '<#> ways to <goal>**

7. **Master the '<#> ways to <goal> and <benefit> in just <timeframe>**

8. The best way to <goal>

9. The best way to <goal> and <benefit>

10. How to stop <problem> with <no. of steps>

11. How to stop <problem> with <no. of steps> in <timeframe>

12. Your shortcut to gain <benefit>

13. Your shortcut to <goal> and <benefit> in <timeframe>

14. Your shortcut to turn your <problem> into <goal>

15. Encounter <no. of steps> to <goal>

16. Encounter the easiest and simplest way to <benefit> and <goal>

17. Encounter the '<#> methods you can use immediately to <benefit>

18. Announcing <no. of ways> you can <benefit>

19. Announcing <no. of ways> you can <benefit> and <goal> easily

20. '<#> types of different methods you can <benefit>

21. Unlock the '<#> secret to <benefit>

22. Unlock the '<#> secret to <goal> and <benefit> in just <timeframe>

23. The top '<#> reasons to <problem>

24. The top <no. of steps> to <benefit> and <goal>

25. The top <no. of steps> to <benefit> and <goal> with <timeframe>

26. Should you still continue to <goal>?

27. Best '<#> tips for <person> to <goal> instantly

28. Are you protecting yourself from <problem>?

29. Looking for <benefit>? Simply read on

30. Improving the <benefit> for <person>

31. The rise of <benefit> and <goal>

32. Top opportunities to <goal> and <benefit> by <timeframe>

33. The do's and don'ts of <goal>

34. <goal> and the importance of it

35. <benefit> and the importance of it

36. Cheapest way to <benefit>

37. Cheapest way to <goal> and <benefit>

38. The fundamentals when it comes to <goal>

39. The '<#> fundamental tips when it comes to <goal> and <benefit>

40. '<#> extra <goal> ideas

41. '<#> steps guide to <benefit>

42. '<#> steps guide to <goal>

43. '<#> reasons why you need <benefit>

44. '<#> reasons why you need to <goal> and <benefit>

45. '<#> breakthrough in <benefit>

46. '<#> breakthrough in <goal> and <benefit>

47. An introduction to <benefit>

48. An introduction to <goal> and <benefit>

49. '<#> creative ideas to <goal>

50. Why you are not <benefit>

51. '<#> guides to successful <goal>

52. '<#> razor-sharp guides for <goal> and <benefit>

53. '<#> truths about <goal> you should know

54. One secret of that they will never let you know

55. Starting <goal> with only a small budget

56. The biggest secret that will cement your <goal> success

57. Can an extra $1000 a month help improve your lifestyle?

58. Why even "beginners" are able to use _

59. How to use the secret of to _

60. The one basic secret of _

61. How to easily pull off _

62. You don't need to create your own _...

63. You don't need to create a _!

64. You don't need to build a list of customers...

65. There is ABSOLUTELY NO _ involved!

66. How to boost _ by up to 30-50%!

67. Why it's actually more simple (and profitable) to _

68. How to get better (and faster) results than _

69. A dirt-cheap, simple do-it-yourself that gives you _

70. A "lazy man's" way to _

71. Secret "2-minute" techniques (that's all it takes!) that

72. New (and simple) that actually _

73. Exactly how and what to _

74. Detailed strategies to _

75. Little-known secrets that can steer you to tremendous _

76. 6 too-simple-to-pass-up ways to _

77. 3 "no brainer" ways to _

78. '<#> steps to be <benefit>

79. '<#> powerful methods to <person> who want to <benefit>

80. '<#> instant working methods

81. '<#> ways to <benefit> and <goal>

82. '<#> ways to <goal> in <timeframe>

83. Building the best <goal>

84. End your worst nightmare now with '<#> sure-fire methods to <benefit>

85. '<#> secrets that only the smart knows

86. '<#> misconceptions about <problem>

87. '<#> misconceptions about <goal>
88. '<#> misconceptions about <benefit>

89. Boost your <goal> by 5 times

90. '<#> of secrets to <goal>

91. Developing the potential to <goal> in you in 2 weeks

92. '<#> important tips to allow you to be <goal>

93. Discover the path to <goal>

94. Discover the truths of <benefit>

95. Discover the secrets of <problem> and overcome them

96. The truth about <benefit>

97. The truth about <problem> you are kept away from till now

98. Imagine you can achieve <goal> in 2 weeks

99. Imagine you can <benefit> in just <timeframe>

100. Imagine you can <benefit> and <goal>

101. At last, you will find out how to <benefit>

102. At last, you will find out how to <benefit> and <goal> in <timeframe>

103. '<#> new tips to <benefit>

104. '<#> new tips to overcome <problem>

105. '<#> new tips to get <goal> within <timeframe>

106. Build your <goal> during recession

107. Harness the secret to <benefit>

108. Harness the secret to <benefit> and <goal> within the next minute

109. '<#> important tools to <goal>

110. '<#> facts about <benefit>

111. Myths about <goal>

112. The #1 myth about <benefit>

113. The #1 myth about <problem>

114. '<#> rules to control <goal>

115. '<#> tips to be <goal/benefit>

116. '<#> sure-win methods to <goal>

117. '<#> strategies I learned from <benefit>

118. The '<#> different ways to <goal>

119. The '<#> habits of <benefit>

120. The silliness of <problem>

121. The rules of <goal>

122. How I changed my life, with <no. of steps>

123. '<#> little things that make <goal> effortless

124. Becoming a god of <goal>

125. Becoming a god of learning <benefit>

126. How to <benefit> more: A <goal> guide

127. The <benefit> that will change your life

128. '<#> ways to turn <problem> into <goal>

129. '<#> shortcuts to finding your <goal>

130. Best <problem> tips ever

131. '<#> clear reasons to <benefit>

132. '<#> clear reasons to <goal> and <benefit> in <timeframe>

133. The '<#> principles of a <benefit>

134. The amazing power of being <goal>

135. The Tao of <benefit>

136. The '<#> productivity tips from a <benefit> master

137. '<#> simple <benefit> fundamentals

138. When willpower is trumped by <problem>

139. Simple daily habits to ignite your passion to <goal>

140. '<#> life lessons from a reluctant <person>

141. '<#> <benefit> lessons for <person>

142. <goal>: '<#> ideas for more <benefit>

143. Finally, the truth about <benefit>

144. Finally, the truth about <problem>

145. Simple <goal> and <benefit> for lazy people

146. How to be <goal> at any age

147. The myth of <goal>

148. '<#> simple tips to deal with <problem> people

149. The really simple way to get <benefit>

150. The really simple way to get <goal> and <benefit> in <timeframe>

151. Get started: From <problem> to <goal>

152. The small-scale approach to <goal>

153. '<#> of lessons I've learnt in '<#> years

154. Breaking free from <problem>

155. The little guide to un-<problem>

156. Surround yourself with <goal> people

157. '<#> mindfulness rituals to <goal>

158. Simple '<#> methods to <goals>

159. For those with burning desire: A <benefit>

160. '<#> essential skills <person> should learn

161. Create the habit of <benefit> and <goal>

162. The <problem> that crush us

163. Your top '<#> questions on <problem>, answered

164. Your top '<#> queries on <benefit>, answered

165. Your top '<#> confusions on <goal>, answered

166. Clearing your <problem> for <event>

167. How to tackle <problem>?

168. How to have the <benefit>?

169. How to have the best <goal> and <benefit> in <timeframe>

170. The <goal> challenge: transform your <problem> in <timeframe>

171. A compact guide to <benefit>

172. A compact guide to your <problem> and turn it into your <goal>

173. The essential <goal> habits

174. '<#> tips for beating the <problem> habits

175. 100 days to <goal>

176. The secret rule of changing <benefit>

177. '<#> simple steps to <goal> from any passion

178. '<#> simple principles for becoming <goal>

179. '<#> simple principles for <benefit> and <goal>

180. '<#> mindfulness rituals to <benefit>

181. The simplest cure for <problem>

182. <benefit>: How to <goal>

183. Can't find a perfect <goal>. Create your own

184. <behavior> like <person>: The first step to <goal>

185. The spiral of <goal>

186. '<#> quick tips to identify <problem>

187. The little book of <problem> remedies

188. The importance of enjoying <benefit>

189. How to be <goal> and still <benefit>

190. '<#> creative ways to avoid becoming <problem>

191. The absolute beginner guide to <benefit>

192. The complete beginner's guide to <goal>

193. The elements of <goal>

194. '<#> ways for <person> to avoid <problem> and <benefit>

195. '<#> ways to combat <problem>

196. How to master the art of <goal>

197. How I became <goal> in about a day

198. How to be <goal>, in under <# of words>

199. Awesome new eBook on <benefit>

200. The truth about _, weekly, etc whether your goal _ or _.

201. Why _, and _ have almost nothing to do with getting _ and _.

202. How to on the Web astonishingly fast ≠ and _

203. Why you could just be one pay check away from financial disaster!

204. 5 steps you can take right now to _!

205. Zero In On The Most Lucrative _ In Minutes.

206. Why You Should Almost Never Use Joint Tenancy To Own Your Assets!

207. Needless _ Later On!

208. 78% Of The TOP _ Shared The EXACT Same Values!

209. You don't need to create your own _...

210. You don't need to create a _!

211. You don't need to build a list of customers...

212. There is ABSOLUTELY NO _ involved!

213. How to boost _ by up to 30-50%!

214. How to Eliminate _ without the use of _.

215. Unleash your body's natural ability to _ from _!

216. Enjoy more free time by knowing _, so you know exactly _.

217. Get instant access to _ that are proven to work

218. Never have to worry about _, _, _ or anything like that, ever again.

219. Baby sleep tricks you haven't tried yet

220. How you can tell he's _

221. Automatically all of your !

222. 20 beauty cheapies for under $10

223. Plain women who attract _-- what have they got?

224. Get happy! Ditch the five things that _

225. Trying for _? A _? How _ can help

226. How to permanently lock your _ into "_"... so you'll never be _

227. cool _

228. Bad _? Can't _? It's not your fault -- here's why, page XX

229. The secret weight-loss spice

230. Broken _ -- the new _

231. things _ should do before they _

232. The very best way to _

233. A smart way to _

234. What _won't tell you

235. How anyone can to .

236. How to secretly and fill it with your _

237. Get the absolute most powerful form of you've ever discovered.

238. A for earning - more from by !

239. How to get busting their guts trying to promote your

240. How To By _

241. Are your _ healthy? Know your risk

242. How to take of just like the professionals do!

243. Harness the secret for .

244. Learn the to manifesting _

245. How To Turn Into _

246. You will be dreaming for this...

247. From bankrupt to millionaire in 3 months...

248. This is why so many people suffering...

249. He has multiple streams of income from...

250. He did it with only 3 hours of work...

Remember these headlines need to catch attention, strike a chord in your audience and lead them into the rest of your copy.

Turn the page to discover how to lead your headline into a juicy sub-headline which will continue to grab their attention.

Chapter 10 – Create a compelling sub-head

So…you have their attention now.

They've been "captured" for the next five seconds.

When the clock hits 6 seconds, what do you do?

Well, your headline has piqued their curiosity, and they're interested in what you're saying, so you'll need to build on it.

Have them tagging along for more.

But how can you do this?

Simple, with a sub-headline.

For example, your headline could say something like:

"EXPOSED: How To Build Desire And Loyalty In Your Relationship"

Your sub-headline could say:

"This is spicing up relationships across the world, having men beg for their women!"

See how it solidifies the headline and makes you want to know MORE?

Your sub-headline is one sentence meant to deliver a HUGE benefit, show proof, give credibility or even add on to the headline.

You can use the sub-headline to give them a taste of what they're about to see.

Show a little credibility, and place yourself as the authority figure by demonstrating some of the results you've seen so far.

Your sub-headline needs to convince your audience to continue reading your advertorial.

If you lose their attention now, the rest of your advertorial is worthless.

Another great way to take advantage of your sub-headline is by giving your audience a WARNING – i.e., "it's something commonly used today – you may even be using it right now!"

Chapter 11 – Stand OUT with a Banner

News flash, being a little "flashy" still catches attention.

By using a banner, especially a different colored one than your headline, will catch the eye and make your website irresistible to your readers.

The hard part is, ensuring your banner is not too flashy, but you don't want it to be too *boring*, either.

There's a fine line in between the two, which is where you want your banner to fall.

How can you create the perfect blend and make your banner attractive to your audience?

Simple, engage with them and tell them to do something with a Call To Action (CTA).

Let me explain.

You see, when your reader stops on your advertorial, they're looking for answers and they're hoping you're going to those to them.

An easy way to get them to engage with your banner is by asking a question, specifically a "yes" question.

This means, your question should supply a "yes" answer from them.

For example, if they're looking to generate new leads you could say,

"Would you like to generate 10 extra leads a day?"

And if you're trying to market the "health niche" then you can say,

"Would losing a few pounds change the way you feel about yourself?"

These types of questions would produce a yes answer and engage with the audience directly asking them about the one problem they want to solve.

While you have their attention, you can try to get them to take action without reading the full page (a good percentage will take this offer, if they really want to solve their problem!).

You can follow up your question with a hyper link, CTA.

For example, a dentist office may want to say some like,

"Looking for the Hollywood smile, without suffering through a fancy procedure? **Click here to see if you're a perfect match for our [INSERT PRODUCT]!**"

The hyperlink will show up as a different color, more often than not it's blue, but it draws attention to the CTA.

This will help drive them to take action and get the answers they've been looking for.

You can also use the banner to include a "WARNING!"

In your advertorial, you may be giving them an insight into something controversial, and you could warn your readers about it.

Or you could use the warning to show them, they may be suffering from something without even knowing it.

For example, if you're in the health niche, you may say:

"WARNING: You may be eating something which is sabotaging your immune system, making you sick without even knowing it. It's more common than you think, and could be a part of your diet right now!"

With this type of warning, we are striking their BIGGEST pain point while showing them it's urgent for them to see this.

Your banner is very similar to your headline and will be one of the first things your readers will see on your page.

You want it to make you look like the authority figure with valuable information, speaking directly to them (one on one) and inspire them to act on your offer.

Once you have your banner, your headline, and your sub-headline…your next step is creating your opening and telling a story.

Don't worry, I'll show you how to do this as well!

Keep reading…

Section 4: How to write a story

Have you ever read a story that just knocked your socks off?

I mean, one where you were hanging on every word…

You couldn't put the book down or close the window to the article until you read every word?

You see, there's a science to it and studies have shown a story is what will keep a person reading for longer than normal.

In fact, stories grab the reader's attention by dropping them into a totally different world than what they're in at the moment.

And I'm about to show you exactly what I'm talking about.

These next couple of chapters, I'll be revealing some great techniques and facts you may not have heard yet about storytelling.

Plus, why it's so important to use storytelling in your advertorial to ensure it's irresistible to your audience.

Chapter 12 – Persuasion with Storytelling

Why is a story important?

I was just talking about how a story can drop you into a whole different world than the one you're in right now...

...and here's what I meant.

You see, as you're reading a story, you start to put yourself in the shoes of the character you resonate with the most.

You imagine what it likes to be a part of the story and how it feels to be there for real.

You can literally place yourself in the scene, have empathy for what the characters are feeling and can't stop reading until you find out what happens to this character you resonate with.

How can you tell a fascinating story?

Simple, show don't tell.

Show them what it feels like to be there, be descriptive about the emotions in each situation, talk about how each character reacted and make your audience feel the emotion like it's their very own.

And the best way to start a story is in the middle of a scene.

Have you ever noticed, every movie begins with an action scene?

One where you're drawn in immediately, wondering why these people are fighting, who are they running from or what in the world is going on.

Either way, your full attention is sucked in, and the movie has you going for another 2 hours.

It's all about the story, how it makes you feel and if you can put yourself in the story somehow.

This is why it works for the movies, and the books.

If you can write an awesome story, then you can charm your way into any readers mind.

You'll be able to tag them along for more, having their complete attention and hanging on your every word.

Example:

> *"Mmmmmm, do you smell that?" I asked my friend, which she obviously didn't hear.*
>
> *As we were walking through the hallway at work, my friend was rambling about her next audit and didn't notice I was no longer following her.*
>
> *You see, I stopped in my tracks, 2 doors ago.*

While she was still walking, I couldn't help myself and inched my way into the room in front of me.

The thing is, I couldn't see right off hand what pulled me into this room.

It was packed with 4 desks with people working and a small room off the back.

Honestly, it was the heavenly smell my nose caught just outside the door, which brought me in.

It smelled of sweet dessert and had my mouth watering.

Frankly, my common sense was on the back burner while my nose and tummy took over.

I asked one of the employees in the room, "what is that amazing smell?"

The guy sitting at the desk by the door told me with a small laugh, "you must be smelling the donuts we brought in this morning." 😄

By this time, my friend realized I wasn't walking behind her and came to see what all the fuss was about.

As she peeked her head in the doorway, she saw me reaching across a desk for a donut, they offered me.

So of course, she had to have one, too.

After asking politely, they said " Yeah sure, you girls better eat them before I eat the whole box. I might not be able to get out of my chair after that."

There goes that little laugh again.

Well, I can honestly say the donut was worth it.

Have you ever had a Krispy Kreme donut?

When the "hot and ready" sign is on, the donuts are freshly baked and still warm.

When you bite into them, they just melt in your mouth with a sugary sweetness.

It's like heaven covered in icing.

Can you smell it? Can you feel it? Can you taste it?

This is what storytelling is for...

...it's to provoke the senses and emotions of your readers.

- Stories help produce Dopamine,
- Which is connected to Pleasure,
- As well as Oxytocin (Rewards),
- And Serotonin (Well-being, Comfort).

Include a story in your advertorial to resonate with your audience and build a relationship with them.

Don't just sell your product, be a good "friend" and talk with them a little while you try to *subtly sell* them.

Once they KNOW you, LIKE you, TRUST you - they will BUY from you and become loyal customers.

Chapter 13 – Where to begin?

The best way to open up an advertorial is with a story.

We've established how a story can make a difference.

But how do you get started, where do you begin the story and what do you say?

Simple.

Think back to the last movie you've seen…

Remember how I said, the really good ones will start in the middle of an "action" scene?

The point is, they all start in the MIDDLE.

They don't start in the beginning, describing every detail of the scene or narrating the beginning of a boring lifestyle.

This wouldn't catch your attention, and it definitely wouldn't make you want to sit there for another 2 hours watching the rest of it, would it?

No.

Picture back to the last time you watch a movie that dragged on… it seemed super slow, right?

So, you'll want to start your opening in the middle of the story.

Just like the story example I've shown you in the _____ before.

Here's where you can take advantage of the fact that you don't have to start off slow and build into the story.

When you start in the middle, you can begin with a scene that pulls on their emotional, heart strings.

(i.e., when your main character is going through a life or death situation or going through a common but devastating experience, etc.)

Why does this work so well?

Well, the thing about starting in the middle of the story is, it gives the reader no opportunity to understand what is going on.

It piques curiosity, demanding they find out what happens next so that they can determine what exactly you're talking about.

However, because of this - it's very "life and death" for your copy to ensure it's interesting and overflowing with emotion.

Openings that are actually captivating make waiting for the explanation thrilling rather than aggravating.

The whole point of the opening is to open the conversation up and lead them into reading the rest of the page.

Make sure it piques curiosity, pulls on their heart strings, and transitions into your offer as smooth as possible.

Here are 5 Simple Ways To Upgrade An OK Story To An Irresistible One!

1) **Go beyond the emotional perspective** – use body language to push past the 5 senses.

2) **Stop striving for PERFECTION** – you may upset people, you may write something controversial, it's may not be the prettiest—and that's ok!

3) **Don't underestimate your audience** – speak at their level, don't belittle them or sound overly intelligent for them.

4) **Use humor when you can** – make your readers laugh, surprise them or catch them off guard with a nice laugh, it helps build a connection with them.

5) **Make them tear up** – whether tears of joy or tears of sadness, this emotion will pull on their heart strings and have them hanging on for more.

Have a story in mind you want to start with?

Follow these techniques and before long, you'll see how easy it to create an incredible story for your audience!

Next up, I'm going to take you through the essential elements of your body copy will need to convert your audience into a subscriber or customer.

Section 5: What should your advertorial say?

You have your audience on the edge of their seats, ready to see what you have to say next, what do you do?

You may know how important a story is, but what should you really talk about?

There are another 11 elements to your advertorial, each one will lead into the next one and take your audience from not sure to more than ready to buy!

Most of these elements are actually, what will make up your story and essentially, make it compelling to your audience.

You see, after you grab their attention, open them up for more, you'll want to continue delivering valuable information.

How can you do this?

Simple, here are the next 7 elements of your advertorials body copy:

- ✓ **Identify WITH Your Audience**
- ✓ **Where They're At**

- ✓ **Where They Want To Go**
- ✓ **Benefits**
- ✓ **AHA! Moment**
- ✓ **Possible Solution**
- ✓ **Your Offer**

Turn the page, and I'll take you through each element plus the 4 additional ones I haven't even mentioned yet.

By the end of this book, you'll have everything you need to create an amazing and compelling advertorial…ready to capture massive amounts of leads for you and convert a good portion into sales!

Chapter 14 – What to say in the body copy?

Element #1: Identify WITH Your Audience

A great advertorial speaks directly to the audience, as if it was written exclusively for their eyes.

The perfect word to portray this feeling is "you, " and you'll want to use it as much as possible, but don't be corny with it.

Act like you're their best friend and just have a conversation with them, on the topic at hand.

If you're using your advertorial like a "case study" you'll want to go about this a different way.

In fact, you'll want the doctor or "authority" figure to resonate and identify with your audience.

This can be done by using real life patient stories or family stories they've experienced which are similar to what your audience is going through at this time.

However, if your advertorial is used like a "raving testimonial," then you'll want it to seem like it's coming straight from their best friend.

Think about it, when you go to a BBQ at your friend's house, complaining about how your grill broke down the day before…

…and he goes on to tell you all about this amazing grill he just bought, then you eat the incredible food made by it and you're practically sold on getting one for yourself.

You didn't see your friend as a salesman, you weren't skeptical from the beginning and you didn't reject his notion because he was just having a friendly conversation.

And the "friendly" conversation just so happened to end in you buying the same grill he was telling you about.

This happens when it comes to movies, health products, household items, and MUCH more.

If you sit there and really think about it, you can probably count at least 2 or 3 times this has happened within the last week to you.

You may not have bought the item, but you've had a friend refer one to you.

The best part is, these are some of the most profitable leads for your business.

How so?

Well, they're warmed up to your topic, introduced to your product and all without having the skepticism normally associated with selling.

They will continue to buy from you until they no longer feel like you're their friend, rather you're a sales person.

Remember to stay, conversational and personal rather than robotic and curt.

Another way to ensure you make them feel like you're their friend is by using the "Us Against The World" method.

This means, you'll have to make them feel like you're on their side and the opposing side will not win.

If you work together, you can dominate…but without you, the other side will take over.

Let's get one thing straight…your audience does not want to hear about you, they want to hear about what you can do for THEM.

Frankly, there's always a certain level of selfishness in the mix.

But lucky for you, you can tap into this selfishness and give them what they're looking for while getting what you want in return.

It's a win-win situation.

And who doesn't love those?

Anyways, when you're trying "identify" with your audience, you want to completely understand who they are.

You'll want to know what makes them tick, why do they do things a certain way, what are they interested in and MUCH more.

You'll want to "become" them, understand how they think and what motivates them.

If you can seem like you've been through the same exact situation or you understand how they're feeling, then they can relate to you.

Once they relate to you, they feel like they have a personal connection with you and your reading their "mind," saying what they've been thinking all along.

Whether it's the hardship they've been through or the goals they're trying to achieve, you can tap into their lives in an emotional way, giving you a stronger bond with your readers.

When you're writing an advertorial, making it from another person's point of view tends to work better.

Let me explain.

You see, when you're walking through the mall and the salespeople standing outside the store tries to stop you…
…you instantly start to withdraw and remove yourself from the situation altogether.

But when your friend comes over, raving about the shopping trip she did last week, you let her in and talk for hours.

She's goes on and on about the amazing results she's seen from the skincare product she bought on that trip.

She's your best friend, you have no reason to be skeptical about it.

So, you give it a try and buy the product yourself.

Who doesn't want to see the amazing results she's seen, right?

Another example is when your friend tells you about this awesome movie they've seen and goes on and on about how you would absolutely love it!

It's more personal than actually watching the trailer yourself.

It's instantly charged with emotion and gives you a connection to the movie without doing it on purpose.

This is how you want your audience to feel.

You want your advertorial to come across as a friend, sharing a new product they've used recently and a good-hearted conversation to go along with it.

See how it comes across as a "glorified" testimonial?

When you give it a personal edge, add a little emotion to it, and make it seem like friendly advice - you'll win them over almost every time!

I mean, you're delivering the solution to all of their problems - make sure they understand, you're there to help.

And they need to feel like they can trust you and you know exactly where they're coming from in order to want more from you.

Test this out for yourself, and go on to discover the perfect way to "walk in your prospects shoes!"

Element #2: Where They're At

Your audience is at a point in their life where they need a "change," but they may not be far enough along, to take the next step yet.

This is where you come in.

You need to walk them through a similar situation to the experiences they are going through right now.

You'll want them to feel like you're reading their minds, your story is straight out of their life and they're not alone.

If they know, you understand what they're going through, they'll open up more and let down the barriers.

For them to take the next step, they'll need to admit they're having a problem, at this very moment.

And it needs to be taken care of before it becomes an even BIGGER problem.

But who really wants to admit they have a problem?

So, it will need to be subtle and encourage them to assess their life, feeling as if…they came up with the idea all on their own.

The best analogy is to "agitate the pain, without rubbing salt in it."

Once they've admitted they have the problem, you can show them there's a solution (your product/service).

The thing is, knocking down their barriers is your main goal.

So, if you can make them feel as if you're their friend and you know where they're coming from, then you have a loyal customer for life.

Element #3: Where They Want To Go

So, you know where they're at, in their lives right this second…

…but do you know where they "want" to go?

Sometimes, they don't even know where they want to go.

They may have a small goal in mind, but most people don't think far enough ahead to have bigger goals.

This is where you can sprinkle in some goals, pushing them in the right direction.

You can use a story to walk them through how their lives, *could be.*

If they want to spend more time with their family, then you'll want to walk them through a story demonstrating MORE, free (happy) time with the family.

If they want to buy a yacht and travel the world, walk them through a story that will give them exactly this.

Element #4: Benefits

This is not where you would leave a bunch of features and hope for the best.

No!

Benefits are a totally different story.

You see, a feature sells the product and a benefit sells what you can get from the product.

For example, if you were to sell a car purely talking about the engine, the style, the sound system, etc.

…versus selling the experience of taking the car to the beach with their family, or a road trip with the best tunes, etc.

See the difference?

In one version, you're selling the features.

In the other version, you're selling the benefits or what they can do with the product.

At our base, humans can be pretty selfish sometimes.

So, while reading your advertorial, your audience will continue thinking – "what will this do for me?"

And this is the question you'll have to answer.

The best way to do this is, by stacking up your benefits and making sure each one is a solution to a problem they're experiencing, at this moment.

They could have a problem making sales, so a few benefits would be:

- ➢ Generating more leads
- ➢ Converting more prospects into sales
- ➢ Creating a residual income
- ➢ The ability to make sales from anywhere

Just remember to talk about how the product can change their lives, and not what the product does itself.

Element #5: AHA! Moment

Have you ever felt like you have an epiphany and this one idea will change your life, forever?

It could have been a moment where you saw someone who had what you wanted, and now your goals are much clearer.

Or it could have been a moment where you were brainstorming, and one idea blew all the other ones, out of the water.

You were excited to see how this will make a difference and ready to put it into action.

There was nothing that could hold you back and nothing could get in your way, you were determined.

And this is what we like to call the "AHA! Moment" where your life story took a turn for the better.

How does this connect with your advertorial?

Simple, after you've walked them through the pain with your story, then you can connect it back to your product with an AHA! Moment.

The turning point in the story where the main character finds the answer to all of their problems.

This is the moment, where you can connect your product/service to the story in a more direct way.

In example:

"I was racking my brain, taking every course, struggling through every training session, and still not seeing any results…

…until one day, when I stumbled across this coach who literally showed everything he knew about _____ and it has changed the way I look at _____."

Your AHA! Moment will lead to your possible solution, which is ultimately – your product/service.

Element #6: Possible Solution

Like I was saying, you'll want to present your product/solution as a possible solution to their problems.

Walk them through how it will solve their problems and what exactly you can do for them.

They need to feel like it's effortless and will deliver massive results.

These days, people want more results with less effort or work to get them.

So, you'll want to make your solution as easy and simple as possible.

You can even walk them through how to use your product/service to make their life better, showing them step by step exactly what they need to do.

Make the work seem like it's a piece of cake and the results are more valuable than the effort it takes to get them.

Be careful about over promising though, it can get you in trouble.

You don't want to promise results, you want to make sure they know the results are "possible" and they could see similar results just like those who have already bought from you.

Element #7: Your Offer

This is IT! This is one of the MOST important elements of your advertorial.

Here is where you would offer your pitch.

Let me explain.

You see, you've already introduced your product/service as a possible solution.

So, they're interested if they're still reading, right?

Well then, here is where you'll want to break down everything they get from you, whether it's a package or just one product with multiple uses.

They need to understand exactly what they're getting out of this exchange and what they need to do to get access to it.

Again, make sure you make it seem effortless and risk-free!

They want to feel like they're getting A LOT out of it without putting much skin into it.

If you're selling something, you'll want to make your price seem like a small investment.

Try not to use the words payment, transaction, and avoid making your price look big like, $49.00 – you can say it like "49 dollars" or "$49" to make it seem smaller and less scary to your readers.

And remember, deliver VALUE, VALUE, VALUE, as much as possible!

If your product/service doesn't deliver as promised or solve problems, then no matter how nice your offer is – your return rate will steadily increase.

They may need another push to ensure they convert, and this is where you can give them some "social" proof.

Element #8: Social Proof

You see, social proof makes it seem like it's real and it's possible they will see the same results. If they're normal, average people just like them, they can do it too – right?

RIGHT!

This goes back to hearing a review from your friend vs. a professional.

Your friend has no alternative motive, no reason to lie to you and absolutely no reason to put you through anything bad.

The skepticism is taken out of the picture and you instantly drop your guard, all your walls crumble like they never existed in the first place.

The same thing happens when you include social proof with your advertorial.

You can share screenshots to social media accounts, a social media comment section, and even testimonials left on your social media feeds.

The more personal it looks, the better!

You see, if they can show your audience that it's possible to see the same results and average people just like them, have seen amazing results, then they instantly feel like they can do it too.

It's like getting on a roller coaster for the first time.

You get the jitters and become a little nervous about it.

But then you see a little 9-year-old girl in the line ahead of you.

And you instantly start to think, if she can do it, then I can do it too!

It tends to make you feel like your own nervousness was foolish and silly to begin with.

All in all, it helps you push past the skepticism you had and help you take the next step in the right direction.

This is what social proof does for your audience.

Throw in as many testimonials or reviews you want!

Then, tell them what the next step is with a CTA (Call To Action).

Element #9: Call To Actions

This element is pretty self-explanatory.
You tell them what to do next to get access, subscribe or invest in your product/service.

Whether you need them to click a button, give you a call, fill out a form or go through a questionnaire...you'll need to tell them what to do or they won't take action.

If your readers are confused in any way, they will start to feel lost and click away from your advertorial.

You want to make sure they know exactly what they need to do to get access.

It's super simple and straight to the point.

Here are a few commonly used Call To Actions:

- ✓ "Click here to get _____"
- ✓ "Click the link below"
- ✓ "Yes! I Want Access!"
- ✓ "Yes! I'm Ready To Get Started!"
- ✓ "You Can Get Started By Clicking The Button Below"
- ✓ And Many, Many MORE!

If they don't take action right away, you can give them a little boost with a "warning" about what happens if they don't buy.

Element #10: What happens if they don't join/buy

If they don't buy or subscribe, you can show them what their life will be like if they don't take action.

Walk them through how their struggles will just increase and get worse by the day.

Show them how each problem they have can lead to another one, and simply destroy their chances of having a happy day.

If it's in the health niche, they could be slowly killing themselves, hacking days off their lives.

Here's where you can over dramatize what they're going through and how horrible it would be if they continued on the path they're already on.

You can stretch it out with worse case scenarios and show them they really don't want to miss out on this!

Element #11: Lock it In With A Guarantee!

Remember when I said you don't want to promise results?
Well, here's where you can work around it.

Normally, you would use a guarantee to promise results and take the risk completely out of the equation.

However, what you would want to do is take the risk out without promising results.

And the best way to do this is by guaranteeing special treatment.

You can guarantee you'll give them your complete attention, treating their problems like they're your own – solving them as fast as possible.

You can guarantee they will get the help they need to make it to the finish line.

The whole purpose of the guarantee is to reassure your prospect and redirect them back to taking action.

50 POWER WORDS YOU CAN USE TO INCREASE THE PULL OF YOUR COPY:

1) Growth
2) Unparalleled
3) genuine
4) free
5) sale
6) special
7) tested
8) improved
9) powerful
10) attractive
11) discount
12) fundamentals
13) valuable
14) how to
15) exclusive
16) superior
17) innovative
18) unlimited
19) confidential
20) reduced
21) unlock
22) authentic
23) practical
24) sensational
25) miracle
26) monumental

27) revolutionary
28) successful
29) wealth
30) insider
31) easily
32) effortlessly
33) simple
34) exploit
35) unconditional
36) secure
37) astonishing
38) promising
39) refundable
40) revealing
41) value
42) gift
43) urgent
44) breakthrough
45) survival
46) quickly
47) luxury
48) unlock
49) exposed
50) quality

Section 6: Know your audience

Why do you go to your friend or someone familiar when you have a problem?

Maybe…it's because, they're always on your side, they give you their full attention and actually, listen to what you have to say?

This is something you want your readers to feel about you (or your speaker).

They need to feel like you're on their side and if it came down to it, you would be right there alongside them through just about anything.

They want to know, you completely understand where they're coming from and will give advice where necessary.

If you can show them, it's you against the world, it will build an unbreakable loyalty in your readers.

Earlier in the book, we spoke about "identifying" your audience, knowing what they like and dislike.

Well, what you're about to read in the next couple of chapters will show you why it's important to secure the bond with your readers and how to make them see, you're on their side!

This will help your advertorial speak directly to your readers, build a connection far deeper than most will ever try for and ensure you have their loyalties for life.

Enjoy!

Chapter 15 – Who does your audience hate?

Why do you need to know who their enemies are?

Simple, if you know if they dislike and why they dislike them, then you can make sure you don't follow in their footsteps.

You want to assure your audience, you're NOTHING like those people.

You know exactly what it likes to be the "outsider" and you're on their side.

They are NOT alone.

Have you ever seen a street fight in the movies?

If one person is pulled into a fight, the whole group backs them up and joins in.

It's about having a crew, feeling safe and knowing you don't have to go through the struggle, alone.

This is how you want your readers to feel.

And lucky for you, they're actively seeking this type of relationship.

They're looking for answers and they want to find someone they can trust enough to believe the answers they give produce.

Ask yourself, if misery loves company, then what does success love?

Success likes to attract other success, and build each other up.

If your audience is looking for results, and you're telling them, you're there for them to help through it all, they'll absolutely LOVE you.

And once they LOVE you, they'll buy from you.

They believe in whatever you have to say.

They'll look at you as not only their friend but also an authority figure who is going to help them out of their dire situation.

So, get to know your audience.

Be a *good* friend, know who their enemies are and have their back through their struggles.

Here are some questions to ask yourself, about your audience:

- ✓ Who are they afraid of?
- ✓ Who makes them feel uncomfortable?
- ✓ Who do they see as competition?

- ✓ Who do they envy?

Each of these questions will help you see a little deeper into your audience's life.

Why do you need to know who they envy?

Simple, if you know who they want to be like, then you can determine how to help them get there.

It's more personal, which in turn helps you seem more real and less "robotic" to your readers.

Plus, it's the best way to build a connection, when you have similar enemies…you can work together to take them down.

Chapter 16 - Are you on their side?

Like I said, you can automatically resonate with your audience, by joining their "side" of things.

When you have a common enemy, it brings you closer together.

You have something to talk about, something to agree on, and something to plan out.

You can join ranks to ensure your enemies never win.

Alone, it would take them twice as long and demands twice as much work from them.

If they have you on their side, they can cut the work and time in HALF.

See where I'm going with this?

Your audience needs to see the big difference in picking you to be on their team.

To dig a little deeper into the "us vs. them" scenario, you'll want to assure them you're nothing like those other people.

How can you do this?

Simple, by telling them how you're so different and what makes you a better "friend" or team member.

Figure out exactly why they hate these people and what makes them an enemy.

Then use this information, to show them you're the complete OPPOSITE.

Walk them through a little bit about yourself, why you choose to be different, and why you are seeing better results.

You could be a fitness coach who believes in one specific routine, and you want to show them how this routine is different than others.

But to show them you're on their side, you'll want to tell them about how your approach fitness may be unusual to them because it's very unique.

Make it a little funny if you need to, laughter has always been my favorite emotion.

You can say something like,

> "I'm not like other trainers…I don't scream at you like a drill sergeant, I won't push to you until you puke, and I definitely don't leave you to your own demise.

My programs revolve solely around you. They're made to cater to your needs, work at a level bearable to you and still show you the results you want.
I promise to treat like you like family, show you the easy way to _____, and never leave you in the dark.

I'm here every step of the way, you're not alone and with me on your side, you'll have everything you need to succeed!"

See how I've reassured them, sprinkled in a little bit about results, and told them they're not alone?

I've made it a little silly with my analogies and boosted their confidence, to feel comfortable enough to make a change.

You see, you'll want them to feel like you're giving them the key to all of their problems without asking for them to put a ton of effort into it.

You're telling them, you'll help them and they won't have to carry the weight of the world all on their own.

If you can get this point across to them, you're golden and your conversions will show it!

Section 7: The turning point

So, I've touched base on grabbing your audience's attention, pulling them in with a story and making sure your story resonates with them specifically…

…now we need to get to the point where you start introducing your product/service, right?

RIGHT!

In this next chapter, you'll discover the best techniques for transitioning your story into your offer without losing your audience along the way.

There is always a way to tie your story back to your product, but the very best way is with an AHA! Moment.

One where your plan falls into place, you can see the goals ahead, and you know where you need to go.

A moment, that makes all the suffering and struggling, worthwhile.

The answer you've been searching for and the solution to all your problems.

And it all hit you like a grand idea, on an average day, after searching for months/years to find it.

Let's begin…

Chapter 17 - The AHA! Moment

The moment that changes EVERYTHING!

This is where you've had an epiphany, the light bulb turns on and you're determined to make a change.

Have you ever felt like you have an epiphany and this one idea will change your life, forever?

It could have been a moment, where you saw someone who had what you wanted and now your goals are much clearer.

Or it could have been a moment where you were brainstorming and one idea blew all the other ones, out of the water.

You were excited to see how this will make a difference and ready to put it into action.

There was nothing that could hold you back and nothing could get in your way, you were determined.

And this is what we like to call the "AHA! Moment" where your life story took a turn for the better.

How does this connect with your advertorial?

Simple, after you've walked them through the pain with your story, then you can connect it back to your product with an AHA! Moment.

The turning point in the story where the main character finds the answer to all of their problems.

This is the moment, where you can connect your product/service to the story in a more direct way.

In example:

"I was racking my brain, taking every course, struggling through every training session, and still not seeing any results…

…until, one day I stumbled across this coach who literally showed everything he knew about _____ and it has changed the way I look at _____."

Your AHA! Moment will lead into your possible solution, which is ultimately – your product/service.
So, you can see now, this is how your story will transition into your offer and ultimately help you convert a larger percentage of your audience.

If you can smoothly take them from reading a story to wanting to your product/service, then you've hit the jackpot!

You'll be able to create an advertorial, hit publish and sit back, while the sales roll in.

Remember the whole purpose of your advertorial is to take your audience from a cold prospect to someone ready to buy from you.

You're warming them up with the story, trapping them with the struggle and pain points they're experiencing...

...all so, your AHA! Moment can come sweeping in to turn the story around for the better.

It shows your audience they do NOT have to stay in the situation they're in.

They CAN get answers, they're life can change and they can become happier!

If you can do it, or your speaker can then they can do it too, right?

Well, this is how they need to feel.

They need to know you can get them out of the slump they're in.

Your AHA! Moment is the moment, they found you.

When they found you, you turned their life around and showed them the way out of the dark tunnel.

You gave them a path to follow, and you were their sunshine on a cloudy day.

Keep this in mind, when you're determining what to say for your story's AHA! Moment.

Section 8: What can you do for them?

Don't sell the features...sell the BENEFITS!

When your audience is reading your advertorial, they don't care about what your product/service as much as they care about what it can do for THEM.

So, get to the point and show them how it will change their life.

Benefits are IMPORTANT, but why are they so important?

Well then, continue reading, because this next chapter is going to walk you this very answer!

Chapter 18 - How can you benefit them?

Your audience isn't interested in what your product/service can do, rather more specifically, what it can FOR THEM.

They want to know, it will give them the change they've been looking for.

If their life has to continue one more day, exactly the way it is now...they may go CRAZY.

So, you're their solution.

Show them how you're going to help, what differences you're going to make and how it will make life easier for them.

This is where most business owners go...wrong.

The most commonly made mistake here is, trying to sell with only features and ignoring the benefits.

You see, a feature shows your audience what a product/service can do, like a smartphone having a flashlight.

On the other hand, a *benefit* will show your audience, how it can change their life.

With a feature, you can describe your product or service, but you can't make your audience picture it as theirs.

You want your reader to instantly WANT your product/service.

And the best way to do this is by using their goals as benefits.

If their goal is to spend more time with their families, then you'll want to use this a benefit.

If they want to look more attractive for their spouses, then this is the best benefit to use for your audience.

Pinpoint exactly what your audience wants, what problems your product/service will solve and create benefits from the mix of the two.

The beauty of using a benefit to sell your product/service is, it does most of the dirty work for you.

Plus, it speaks directly to your audience, pulling strings, and triggering their deepest desires.

You want them to feel like you're giving them the magic pill, without over promising on results or outcomes.

That's where showing your case studies as "social" proof will work in your favor.

You see, their main goal is to reduce stress, solves problems that are causing their life to be a huge mess.

If you can help smooth it all out, and show them people are already seeing some amazing results, then you have them HOOKED.

Don't forget to *show* them how you can change their lives and don't just tell them about your product/service.

Section 9: Credibility

Ready for the next step?

You see, you can always link your advertorial to your social media accounts and create a following from it.

If you want them to join a group or like your page, you can always include those buttons in there.

This next section will break down each type of link you may want to use and why it would help your business in the long run.

Plus, you'll see the reason for including social proof and reassuring your audience with real life credibility.

Now, turn the page and discover more about creating a compelling "social" proof section.

Chapter 19 – Give PROOF

Social proof is your credibility and it can either boost your sales or cut your conversions.

It all depends on looking real, not sounding fake and showing them your product/service actually works for just about anyone.

Think about it, when your friend comes up, raving about an awesome movie they just saw and recommended you go see it right away…

…you're going to go see it, right?

And this is why social proof works!

If someone on Facebook gives you an impressive testimonial, you can post it

Check out these two statistics revealed by consumer research around American consumers: [from kissmetrics]

1. Over 70% of Americans say they look at product reviews before making a purchase. [source]
2. Nearly 63% of consumers indicate they are more likely to purchase from a site if it has product ratings and reviews. [source]

For example, when you're looking for a movie to see in the theater, you don't just watch the trailer...

...you also, read through the reviews and probably even ask a few friends if it's any good.

It's natural to want someone else's opinion on something before making a serious decision about it.

It takes most of the responsibility off of them.

You see, social proof makes it seem like it's real and it's possible they will see the same results.

If they're normal, average people just like them, they can do it too – right?

RIGHT!

This goes back to hearing a review from your friend vs. a professional.

Your friend has no alternative motive, no reason to lie to you and absolutely no reason to put you through anything bad.

The skepticism is taken out of the picture and you instantly drop your guard, all your walls crumble like they never existed in the first place.

The same thing happens when you include social proof with your advertorial.

You can share screenshots to social media accounts, a social media comment section, and even testimonials left on your social media feeds.

The more personal it looks, the better!

You see, if they can show your audience that it's possible to see the same results and average people just like them, have seen amazing results, then they instantly feel like they can do it too.

It's like getting on a roller coaster for the first time.

You get the jitters and become a little nervous about it.

But then you see a little 9-year-old girl in the line ahead of you.

And you instantly start to think, if she can do it, then I can do it too!

It tends to make you feel like your own nervousness was foolish and silly to begin with.

All in all, it helps you push past the skepticism you had and help you take the next step in the right direction.

This is what social proof does for your audience.

Throw in as many testimonials or reviews you want!

Then, tell them what the next step is with a CTA (Call To Action).

Chapter 20 - Why you need a group

Have a Facebook group where your customers can link up and build a community around your product/service?

Then you should probably create one.

It's free and simple.

It takes less than 10 minutes and will give you the perfect place to build a list of people who will buy up anything you put in front of them.

Especially, if they're already buyers.

You see, nobody wants to be alone or do anything difficult, by themselves.

It's always better when you have friends, who will do it with you.

With this in mind, you can create a Facebook group where all of your customers can get together and give advice, ask questions, or just feel like they're a part of a community.

And it's really easy to add members to your group.

All you have to do is, link your Thank You page with your Facebook group and invite people to join your tight-knit community.

You can also sprinkle a sentence into your advertorial, mentioning the fact…you have a group where they can go to be with like-minded people, who will help them grow and push them over the finish line.

Once you have a few people in your group, you can get the point where you don't even have to post in there on a daily basis.

Your members will post, other members will create conversations, and even some of them will generate motivation for the others.

You can even find a few mediators who will volunteer to help you manage the group and ensure everyone gets along, post for you to keep engagement up and even message for you, so you don't have to reply to every message yourself.

 A group could only benefit your business and give you a pot of buyers to dip into when you have a new promotion or deals going on.

What are you waiting for? Create your group, right now!

Chapter 21 - Get more page likes

You can link your advertorial to many things.

For example, you can link your advertorial to a sales page.

Or you can link it to a One Time Offer page.

You can even link it directly to an order form.

Maybe, even link it to your blog site.

It all depends on what you want your funnel to do.

Your funnel could just be for lead generation.

In this case, you would want to keep your audience's attention as long as possible and keep them in the circle of "content."

Let me explain.

If you already have your reader's attention, you promise a lead magnet and they give you their contact information to get the lead magnet…what do they do next?

Do you want them to click away immediately and visit your email to look at the lead magnet?

Or would you like to keep their attention on your funnel at the time being?

You see, it's all about what you're looking to do with your funnel.

If you looking to make sales from your advertorial, you can link it to an order form or send them to an upsell to add more to their cart.

Frankly, if you want to "safeguard" their attention and ensure they're only thinking about your products/services, then you'll want to keep them in your funnel for as long as possible.

So, link your advertorial to a sales page, article, newsletter, one-time offer and even more!

Remember, stay relevant and if they like one product/service, they may like another one if it's similar or has a similar benefit.

Chapter 22 – Testimonials sell themselves

A testimonial sells your product/service for you.

If someone has already seen amazing results and is willing to tell the world your product/service is amazing, then it seems it may be worth it to your reader to give it a try.

It makes it seem more possible, and the results are a solid thing now.

You see, a testimonial can eliminate the skepticism your audience has towards, whether or not your product/service works.

It's literally the first thing they're going to think when you start to offer your product/service.

Think about it, the last time you went to see a movie…was it just because of the trailer?

Or did you look at a couple reviews and hear your friends mention it a few times?

You see, when someone mentions how amazing a movie was, it instantly catches your attention.

Why?

Simple, because they're not a salesperson and they aren't trying to push anything on you.

This means, your walls are down, and you absorb what is being said to you.

Well, this is what you want your readers to feel.

You'll want them to give you their full attention, feel comfortable enough to invest with you and feel secure in the idea – your product/service can change their life.

If someone as average and common as they are, could see results from it – then they can too!

It makes it seem like a smaller challenge with the likelihood of seeing even more results without giving an arm and leg.

Show them people are already happy with their results, seeing a difference in their lives, and prove your product/service works!

Section 10: What do you have to offer?

So, you have a story and your audience is HOOKED.

What's next?

How do you transition them into buying from you or subscribing to your list?

Simple, you'll want to introduce your offer.

Show them what they get from it, how it will change their life and persuade them to take action.

But before you freak out, read this next chapter and discover how to introduce your offer without repelling your audience for good.

Chapter 23 - Introduce your offer (pitch)

A sales pitch in disguise…

Again, people do NOT like being sold, they'll go out of their way to avoid salespeople!

With this in mind, your content must not look sales-y or to corporate looking.

You can even use some of the news websites and popular blogs to pinpoint the look that's working with your audience right now.

It helps to ensure your readers can easily scan and follow along with your copy.

This means, breaking up large sections and creating BOLD sub-headlines to help keep the readers' eyes comfortable.

But remember, you want to give more value than you take. So, keep any sales talk until the very end, where you subtly ask for them to take action.

If they've read your advertorial this far, they're interested in what you have to offer.

They want to see if you have all the answers and if it's within their "budget" to get them.

You have to make your offer seem like you're delivering more value which is worth WAY more than what you're asking for it.

Plus, keep in mind words like payment, transaction, or cost will repel your audience and turn them off from the sale.

You'll want to make it seem like it's an investment because no matter what you're offering, they are looking to invest in themselves.

Your product/service is the answer to their problems and they're just looking to invest in making their life better.

If you can make the investment look like it's chump change compared to the way their life will be about they buy, then you have them in the bag.

You're GOLDEN.

Another great way to make your price seem like it's a piece of cake, is by showing an "original" price and showing a discounted price.

For example, if your product is $197, show it like: "$475 Now Only $197!"

Everyone loves to get a discount, even if they aren't really getting one.

They will think they were saving money and got the best deal.

Plus, if you flood it with value then your price is even smaller in their minds.

It's just another way of making your product/service irresistible to your readers.

Don't forget to keep the corny and cheesy phrases out of the equation.

You want them to feel comfortable with you, trust you and eventually, buy from you (over and over again)!

And the BEST way to make your product/service look even better is by loading it up with "freebies."

Turn the page to discover what types of freebies will help your readers convert, almost effortlessly.

Section 11: Give more than you get

Did you ever go to a meeting, where one person charged in demanding for attention and requesting everyone do as they say?

Were you excited to stand up and do what the person said?

When you demand action with nothing in return, no incentives, no appreciation, and no consideration for the other person – then you won't get what you want and they won't "happily" do as you say.

This goes for just about anything in life or business.

You have to be willing to give a little, to get a little in return.

The best way to do this is by giving your audience a freebie!

Yes, I do mean, you're giving them something for absolutely NO money in return.

Why?

Simple, you want them to appreciate you, trust you and see you're there to help them.

After they feel this way towards you, then they're ready to buy from you.

This next chapter will show you just how important it is to include a freebie in your plans.

If you don't, you'll be sabotaging your business and killing your chances of success.

Chapter 24 - Why you NEED a freebie

The best way to warm someone up to you is by giving them something for free.

Think about it, even most restaurants give you a complimentary started dish like bread or chips.

It's to hold you over, keep you happy and increase the value of the restaurant in your eyes, as the consumer.

It's all about appealing to the needs of your audience.

If you can help them out without asking for an arm and a leg in return, they'll think you're the most generous person they've ever met.

So, when you get to the point of asking for money, they'll feel like you've given them so much already, they're confident whatever you're offering is worth the money.

Seriously, who doesn't like to be given free stuff?

When your reader lands on your advertorial and it offers free stuff, it's kind of like Christmas day and your readers are getting a gift/present.

And when you ask for their contact info, they'll think it's such a small price to pay to get the free gift from you.

Well, as long as your freebie is valuable and not useless.

You may have heard of a "lead magnet" but never quite understood what it was.

But really, it's just a freebie you're giving your lead in return for giving you their contact info.

It's a magnet for your leads, get it?

Anyways, the best way to ensure your lead magnet is irresistible is by giving them a taste of what you have.

You can use a free report, eBook, or cheat sheet to give them a taste of the answers you have and the results they could get access to.

If you deliver a freebie which actually generates results for them, then they'll definitely come back for more – excited to see what else you have!

Your lead magnet could consist of a template or a routine to follow.

Giving them a step by step plan to act on, taking away the confusion and showing them the right path to mirror.

It doesn't matter if you're in the health niche, self-development, financial, or beauty niche…any audience will LOVE to receive something for free.

You could give a sample of your product or a free service as a starter.

You can even give them access to the tools you use, or the resources you have.

It doesn't have to be an eBook or report.

There's plenty of things you can use as a lead magnet and your audience will fall head over heels for your products.

Don't limit yourself, think outside the box and be a little creative.

You don't have to follow in the footsteps of your competition.

You can create a new path.

It wasn't long ago, people would have looked at you crazy if you mentioned a "webinar."

But now, they're used as a freebie lead magnet as well!

Think about it.

Your options are endless!

Section 12: What is it worth?

Have you heard about the 80/20 rule?

Well, this rule is where you give your prospects 80% value and 20% pitch.

But even in your pitch, you want to be delivering a ton of value.

The easiest way to do this is by stacking your products/services to make it look like they're getting 100 things for the price of 1.

Make sense?

Then turn the page, and let's dive right in.

This next chapter will break it all down for you!

Chapter 25 - How to increase your value

You've probably heard someone at some time say, "I'm on a budget."

But what they're really saying is, I don't see the value in what you're offering.

They think it's not worth the money and therefore they've put themselves on a budget to worm you down to a *lower price*.

A better way to reverse this and ensure you close your audience *no matter the price* is by **overpacking it with value.**

You want your audience to feel like they're getting $1M dollars-worth of valuable stuff from you **for only 50 bucks.**

They want to know, you're there for them…and dip after, you've taken their money

They need to see, you're not going to give them the first couple steps and leave them there, wondering where to go to next.

They want to know that you're going to give them more than their dollar's worth and they need something to give them a reason to not even blink at the price you give them.

How can you increase your value?

It's pretty simple, and I'll explain each one for you.

The most obvious route, and uncommonly taken, is by increasing your price to show you are a higher value item.

Think about it, people buy "brand name" products even when they're more expensive.

Why do they continue to buy them?

Well of course, it's the boost in status the brand name items give them.

It's the looks they get from people, the compliments they get from their friends and the uplifted mood from feeling "popular" or attractive to the world.

Or you can get a "knock off" and be looked at as *cheap*...which would you choose?

So, by simply increasing your price – you've established yourself as a higher quality of products/services and in the end, you'll attract a higher quality of leads from it.

You can also make it more convenient to get and use your product/service.

Let me explain.

You see, if you make it easier for them to buy and use your product/service, most of the work is taken out of the equation for them.

If you're giving them a step by step plan, they no longer have to test out other plans – they can follow yours and cut the stress out of the situation.

Why is perceived value so important?

Frankly, if your value is greater than your price tag, your customers are more likely to buy and want more of your products/service.

It's all about, giving the customers what they want and making it seem like such a tiny investment to get the results they want.

Another way to increase your value is by packing it with bonus or freebie content.

You could throw in a cheat sheet, a video training course, an eBook, etc.

Your audience LOVES to receive more than what they're paying for.

So, if you make it seem like, just because they're on your page at this very second...they will also get bonus items ON TOP of everything else for FREE!

Who doesn't like FREE stuff?

Look, we both know you're really just trying to decrease the fears of your readers.

You see, there a diehard skeptic and their looking for ANY reason to brand you as a scammer.

To avoid this mess altogether, you'll want to increase the value of your product/service and deliver more than you're asking for.

The easiest way to do this is with:

- ✓ Money Back Guarantees
- ✓ Testimonials
- ✓ Video Demos
- ✓ Free Trials
- ✓ Show Them Your Authentic & Genuine
- ✓ Compare yourself to more expensive options

Don't forget, your reader is looking to find a reason to NOT like you – don't give them the chance to find one.

Make them LOVE you by *overdelivering on value* and asking for very little in return.

Section 13: Secondary content

What's the column next to your advertorial for?

Well, this is what we call the "sidebar" and it's your best opportunity to link other pages to your advertorial.

There are so many things you can include in your sidebar, where to begin…

These next few chapters will walk you through some sidebar tactics you can use to take advantage of the attention you already have from your prospects.

If they're already on your page, you might as well use this time to point them to another one of your pages.

However, it's NOT always about making sales from it.

You could just be generating leads from it or pushing them to your friend's site, either way – your sidebar is the perfect chance to keep your audience hanging on.

Turn the page and let's get started!

Chapter 26 - How can you use a sidebar?

What's amazing about the side bar, is the opportunity to keep your audience in your "circle" and engaging with your business in one way or another.

When I say "circle" I'm talking about anything that has to do with your business, this can be an article, access to more products, the chance to sign up for more valuable information, etc.

It could be another funnel or website altogether, or it can be another page in the same funnel.

This is a way to hold your audience's attention and give them more reasons to LOVE you.

The more you GIVE, the more they LOVE you, the more they'll BUY from you.

Here are just a few of the ways you can use the sidebar to your advantage:

- ➢ You can include an opt-in form in the sidebar

- ➢ You can include pictures with hyperlinks to your blog site

- You can include links to *relevant* affiliate products

- You can include an "about me" to introduce yourself a little more in depth

- You can include your social proof or references in the sidebar

- You can include a link for feedback and questions in the sidebar

You see, your sidebar is important - it's not a place to leave cluttered like a 3-year old's bedroom.

You want it to look organized, show the sites or items you want to feature and encourage action from your audience.

In fact, your sidebar is the secondary content to your advertorial.

It's not the MAIN focus, but it can encourage your audience to take action and stay within your business' circle.

It's basically there to fuel your audience to interact with your business a little more.

Building a stronger bond with them, warming them up even more to invest with you sometime, in the near future.

So, remember to be unobtrusive with your sidebar and stay relevant to what your advertorial is talking about.

You don't want to confuse them or repulse them with things they have NO interest in.

In these next couple of chapters, I'm going to dive deeper into each type of content you can include within your sidebar to interact with your audience on another level.

Chapter 27 - Link to a blog site

Keeping your audience on your website and gobbling up your content is the best way to build loyalty.

If you want them coming back for more, then keep delivering valuable information.

The easiest way to do this is by linking your advertorial with more content in the sidebar using articles.

Sometimes, what we see as something so "basic" could actually be brand new to someone who's reading your articles.

So, you can do something simple like a "How To" or "7 Steps To" and show some of the basics in your niche.

The best way to see what's "Trending" in your niche and what will grab attention, is by visiting some of the online magazines in your niche.

For example, there's the women's health magazine, Forbes, Entrepreneur, etc.

You can check out the headlines that are currently working, and what topics are catching people's attention.

This gives you a better idea of how your article or blog should look.

Here's a Simple 6 Step Formula For Writing An Attractive Article

- ✓ **Step #1:** Headline
- ✓ **Step #2:** Story/Value
- ✓ **Step #3:** Bullet
- ✓ **Step #4:** Bullet
- ✓ **Step #5:** Bullet
- ✓ **Step #6:** Conclusion/Call To Action

You see, with an article you would still want them to take action.

Whether you want them to go to another article, subscribe or give feedback…

…you'll want to tell them exactly what you want them to do.

Chapter 28 - Lead them to a sales page

Have relevant products or services your audience may be interested in?

This is the best opportunity to take advantage of already having their attention.

They're already interested in what you're saying, trust that you're saying the right stuff and believe you're delivering value that they can use.

So, of course, this is the best time to market your products/services.

Coordinate your picture hyperlink or headline with the same headline on your sales page.

The familiarity of seeing both headlines the exact same will catch their attention more than using two different styles of headlines.

It's a great way to link your advertorial with your sales page and to ensure there's traffic visiting your page.

Especially if your audience is already warmed up to you.

This will increase your chances of converting them into sales if they're already interested in what you're saying.

And if they've bought from you once, they're even more likely to buy from you again.

If you have relevant products/services to the topic at hand, then you should definitely promote them in the sidebar of your advertorial.

This also helps your advertorial look like a real article or news clipping.

And increases the authority of your site, making you look even more like an expert because you're "connected" with so many other pages.

Chapter 29 - Promote affiliate products

Maybe you don't have products/services of your own.

NO WORRIES.

There are plenty of people who will give you complete access to sell their products/services and even give you a cut of the profits.

No need to build your own or spend countless hours tweaking to perfect it.

It's completely done for you.

All you need to do is market it.

And what better place to market it than on your advertorial where you already have their attention and what you're talking about is relevant.

It's super easy and gives you the opportunity to sell without being in their face with it.

It's just on the side, asking for their attention if they want to give it.

Very subtle, and more personal than being sold with more hype and demands.

The probability of selling to an existing customer is 60 – 70%. The probability of selling to a new prospect is 5-20% – Marketing Metrics.

Where can you go to find these products/services?

Simple, check out JVZoo.Com or ClickBank.Com to see if there's a product/service relevant to your niche.

The best part about it is, most of the business owners on there will give you what you need to market their products/services.

They'll give you emails, banner ads, Facebook ads, sales pages, and even keywords to use in your advertorial to ensure it's all related.

This just makes it easier than ever for you to promote just about anything you want without creating a product yourself.

It's pretty "cookie-cutter" and easy to implement.

Amazon even lets you become an affiliate as well!

You could be talking about school, how to maximize your studying and promote a backpack from Amazon.

In fact, Amazon will give you a percentage of the sale just because you promoted it for them.

This works in more ways than one and gives you a boost to generate a few extra dollars each month.

Section 14: What actions do they take?

You can create an amazing story, one that has your audience on the edge of their seats, desperate to read what comes next.

But your readers won't become a lead unless you tell them what you want them to do.

Don't worry, I'll walk you through the best techniques for doing just this!

In fact, here's what this section reveals:

> - How To Create *Magnetic* Call To Actions – Ones to stand out, grab attention and motivate your prospects to take action
> - How To Successfully "Sell" From Your Advertorial – Without pushing your prospects away by sounding corny and too hyped up
> - And Much MORE!

Take your time and give these next couple of chapters your full attention, especially if you want to convert your audience into a subscriber or customer.

Chapter 30 - CTAs (Call To Actions)

If you don't tell your audience exactly what you want them to do, then you can't expect them to take action in any way.

It would be like, you just wrote a blog instead of an advertorial.

You see, a blog just informs and gives your audience something to learn from, without feeling like they're in school.

Your advertorial is supposed to do this too, AND it needs to convince them to give you their contact information while pushing them to the sale.

The whole point of your advertorial is to be subtle by being more personal with them, but you still need to include an action for them to take.

Again, if you don't tell them what you want them to do then they'll mosey on their way and you'll miss the opportunity to collect another lead.

A great "subtle" way to push them to take action is with a hyperlink.

The cool thing is your hyperlink can be ANYTHING.

You can tell them to click here or click below with it.

Or you can use the words already in your sentence like [this one](), and hyperlink it.

Here are some proven stats by many well-known marketers, to think about when it comes to your CTAs:

1. [ContentVerve]() saw a 90% increase in click-through rate by using first-person phrasing: "Start my free 30-day trial" vs. "Start your free 30-day trial."
2. Helzberg Diamonds saw a 26% increase in clicks by adding an arrow icon to their CTA buttons. ([Marketing Tech Blog]())
3. SAP found that orange CTAs boosted their conversion rate over 32.5%. ([QuickSprout]())
4. Performable found that red CTAs boosted their conversion rate by 21%. ([QuickSprout]())
5. Making CTAs look like buttons created a 45% boost in clicks for CreateDebate. ([Copyblogger]())
6. Personalized CTAs convert 42% more visitors into leads than untargeted CTAs. ([HubSpot]())
7. Neil Patel found that users prefer to learn about the offer before clicking a CTA -

placing his CTA above the fold decreased conversions by 17%. (QuickSprout)
8. Reducing clutter around their CTA increased Open Mile's conversion rate by 232%. (VWO)
9. FriendBuy increased signups by 34% by adding anxiety-reducing content and explaining key benefits next to their CTA. (Copyblogger)

Just keep in mind, what works for other people - may or may not work for you.

Don't be upset when something doesn't show you the exact results someone else saw.

Continue testing, you'll find what works best for your specific business needs.

To become a super successful CTA, you'll need to do some A/B testing, and have an open mind to think outside the box, trying new things as much as possible.
Against popular belief, it's a great idea to split test even when you're seeing some pretty good results.

Your results can always improve. Plus if you find the one small key to massive improvements then you've hit the jackpot and the testing was worth it!

Chapter 31 – Lead generating CTAs

How would you use a "Call to Action" without asking for money or selling anything?

For a business to run solely online and be a huge success, it needs a long list of email subscribers.

With this in mind, you'll need a call to action, but you're not asking for money.

So, the "close" in this situation is, getting their personal contact information.

Why do you need their contact information?

Well, once you have a long list of email subscribers, you can promote any of your products/services through your emails.

On average, you can make about $3 per subscriber per month, especially if you're sending emails on a regular basis and delivering a ton of value.

The key to using your advertorial as an "opt-in" generator, is to ask the right way for their info.

You see, people like to keep their personal info close to their hearts and not share it with anyone.

Or so they think.

And this is where the skepticism comes in…

You better have a great reason for them to give you their info.

What better reason, than to get access to something they want.

It can be a book on something they want to learn, a report showing they what to avoid, it can be access to a newsletter, free tickets to an event, etc.

You have infinite options when it comes to giving a "freebie" to your audience.

You can even make it a contest, where they join the contest for an opportunity to win something that is relevant to your product/service.

You can also, give them a sample of your product/service for free, as a trial.

I've compiled a few "CTAs" either I've used or someone else has used and seen some success from them.

You can analyze what makes them work, use them as your own (after you edit them to make them uniquely yours) and remember to test what works best for your audience.

Here are a few ways to get to take action:

> ➤ "Discover The Key To _____, In Your Inbox, Almost Immediately!"
> ➤ "Getting Access Is As Simple As, Filling In The Box Below And Clicking The Button!"
> ➤ "Don't Worry About Suffering From _____ Any Longer, After Downloading Our _____ _____, You'll Be Saying Goodbye To Those Pesky Problems For Good!"
> ➤ "Now, don't waste any more time, click the button below and get started right away!"
> ➤ "We look forward to having you, click the button and join us for our _____"
> ➤ "Want to get this consultation for free? Then you'll want to act fast and see if we have any appointments available right now!"
> ➤ "Join us for exclusive access to _____ and never go through this alone again!"
> ➤ "Yes! I want to get access for free!"
> ➤ "I'm ready to get started right now!"

As you can see, some of the CTAs tell the audience to click on something but other push them in the direction of taking action without directly saying it.

Some can be subtle, and others can be more forceful.

It depends on what works for your particular audience.

And your button would look slightly different than your CTA.

You may want it to say,

"Yes! I want what you're offering!"

Which is an "identifier" for your reader and makes them admit they want what you have.

If they click on the button, they are more likely to go through with the purchase than someone who clicked a button that said,

"Order Here!" or "Subscriber HERE!"

It's less personal and doesn't speak to your audience at all.

Also, I would like to share some additional techniques you can use to ensure your advertorial converts readers into subscribers.

10 Lead Generation Techniques You'll Want To Follow To See Massive Results:

    1) Place your call to actions before the fold

2) Images stand out more than text according to heat map studies

3) Call to action button colors should contrast with the rest of the site color scheme

4) Use hyperlinks and place CTAs on the most relevant pages,

5) Connect the CTA headline to the corresponding landing page headline

6) Plainly state what your reader will get if they click on the CTA

7) Include your opt-in forms above the fold – and keep them as simple as possible

8) Use images to show what you are offering – images capture the eye much faster

9) Use bullets to emphasize your benefits

10) Get rid of the navigation elements & extraneous links

Bonus Tip*** Include a "thank you" page to keep the lead engaged and restore the navigation menu for your "thank you" page

Section 15: Push them over the edge

So, you've made your offer, and they haven't taken action yet.

What do you do?

Simple, load them up with a little bit of scarcity.

Admit to them, they could be left behind if they don't take action now.

You see, your reader is on the edge of their seat and here's where they decide…whether or not, to go for it.

If they feel like your product/service is in high demand, they'll want it just so they can be like everyone else.

But if they're on the fence, they may need to be pushed a little to make the decision.

When you turn the page, you'll read about "injecting scarcity" into your advertorial and ensure your audience converts into sales.

Chapter 32 - Persuade them with scarcity

You need to push them over the edge.

Give them an irresistible reason why they should take action, right this second, rather than waiting.

This is the moment, the one where your audience still has some doubts and you'll need to reassure them.

They could either turn around, ignore everything they've read up until then and hightail it to something else, more interesting than your advertorial.

Or you could light a fire under their butts to push them to feel the urgency of the situation.

Supply => Demand

If your product/service is in high demand, it increases the value of it.

Here's what I mean…

If your prospect reads through an amazing testimonial for how amazing your product or service is, they're at the point where they HAVE to have what you're selling.

Then when you throw a curveball, telling them there are only 5 left - they instantly go into desperation mode, and they can't LIVE without your product/service.

==They act much faster when they think they could miss out on this amazing opportunity you're presenting them.==

It comes down to the element of ==TIME -== and knowing they can't wait a second longer or they'll be left behind.

Let's be frank==, NOBODY== likes to be left behind.

There's plenty of ways to light the fire under their seats and drive them to make a move.

Let's brainstorm for a second,

You can always say things like, "we only have enough spots for 5 people, so if you're the 6th person I'll have to turn you away…and I definitely don't want to do this. Let's make sure you don't get left behind and get started right now by_____…"

If they feel like you have the answers to their problems, then they definitely don't want to be left out.

They could continue suffering and experiencing a life of hell or they could invest in your offer.

Since your product/service is in high demand, they want to be a part of the club as well.

They don't want to be the loner who's kicked out to the curb just because they didn't sign up fast enough.

They don't want to be laughed at or ridiculed because they weren't included.

It's like being the person who doesn't keep up with current events and doesn't realize their town is on fire because they don't watch the news or listen to their emergency alerts.

Your reader doesn't want to be this person…nobody actually wants to be this person, it's normally a result of bad luck or terrible planning.

So, trigger this emotion in your reader and inject scarcity into your advertorial to ensure they convert into a customer or subscriber.

Section 16: How can you reassure them?

If your reader hasn't taken action this far in the advertorial, then they're on the fence about it.

You need to reassure them and make them feel comfortable with you again.

It's all about persuading them, your product/service is the answer to their prayers.

It's the miracle they've been looking for.

And if they need to feel like it's a risk-free investment.

They are handing over money to you, and they want to feel like it's MORE than worth it for them.

The best way to do this is with a guarantee, and I would even recommend using multiple guarantees.

I once used over 7 guarantees in one sales letter.

And this next chapter will walk you through creating a GREAT guarantee!

Chapter 33 – Name your guarantees

The key to a great offer is making it a "risk-free" decision.

And the best way to do this is by filling it with an irresistible guarantee.

You want your prospects to feel like the risk is all on you, even if they're not the type to ask for a refund.

It's essential for your guarantee to be completely honest and transparent to your readers.

You want them to know they have a certain amount of time, to return it.

Plus, if they don't like it for some ungodly reason, they can get their money back.

But follow this up with a confidence booster.

For example, you can say:

"However, I'm 100% confident you're going to absolutely love the {INSERT PRODUCT NAME} and the results you'll see from it."

It's ok to include the sentences you may think are a little negative like the one saying they can get a refund.

You see, if you follow up a negative with a positive, then your audience will only think of the positive.

In fact, they'll forget the negative things you talked about almost instantly, it's all in the short-term memory and the need to hear what they want to hear.

If you've reassured them, then they can completely move on from the downside and look at the bright side in things.

At this point, your audience may be on the fence about your product/service.

They were just introduced to it, and they're not fully sold.

I mean, they've already heard your offer, seen your social proof, and there's still something holding them back.

A guarantee can be the breaking point, the one thing that pushes them over to your side of the fence.

If you can reassure them, demolish their skepticism, and destroy their rebuttals, then you're golden.

You want them to feel comfortable with you, trust you, see you as a friend and someone who is on their side.

Your guarantee can portray this, or it can make them feel like you're just slapping it on there to make them feel better.

You don't want to be cheesy with it, and you definitely don't want to, just slap a badge on there and hope it just a great job.

A great guarantee will show your reader, you're there for them, you'll treat them like they're special goods and they have you there to make sure they don't stray from the path.

Remember, you're trying to solve a problem they're experiencing right now.

Most problems tend to look like a HUGE obstacle and tend to look scary.

You can use this to reassure them, they're problem is easy to overcome and you have the solution for them.

They need to feel like you know what you're talking about, you have their needs in mind and you treat them like they're family.

Normally, your reader has been scorned or burned by someone like you in the same niche.

They may be thinking you're just like them.

This brings us back to the "Us VS Them" scenario. You need to reassure them you're not just there for their money.

You're there to help them see results, you're in it to win it, and their results will be treated like they're your own.

You've got this, now give it a try!

Section 17: How should it all look?

I wouldn't just leave you with all of this information and hope you make it on your own.

Everything I've shown you so far has been used one way or another for projects I've written for my clients.

I would never steer you down the wrong path or try to make things harder for you.

With this in mind, I would like to show you a few samples I've written recently.

You see, each advertorial is different, but they follow the same formula.

You'll notice the pattern when you turn the page to the next section!

Chapter 34 - Advertorial samples

Well, I've already walked you through how to write a persuasive advertorial…

…now, I would like to show you how they actually look when they're put together.

Turn the page to get a look at some pretty awesome advertorials you can swipe and use for inspiration!

~ SAMPLE 1 ~

BEGINNER TRADERS: How To Turn $1 Into $100 Through Currency Trading

...And Get The Inside Scoop Into What Markets Are Best To Invest In Right Now!!

Are you tired of trying to juggle the markets and actually generate *steady* profits?

This isn't something to be embarrassed about, it's more common than you think for traders to get overwhelmed in the beginning.

Especially when they don't have someone to help them through it.

You see, when it comes to learning the "ins and outs" of global trading, it can get a bit confusing.

Frankly, it takes years of studying the charts, analyzing the data, and a bit of "trial and error" to start seeing *good* results with your investments.

Before you start to worry, there *are* ways to consistently make money trading currencies.

Most people just "don't know, what they don't know" and never crack the code which could earn them millions.

The thing is, to make money and become successful trading currency, requires having someone on the inside. Someone with the experience, proven strategies and knowledge to help you predict the markets with minimal losses and maximized profits.

<Insert Direct Response Banner>

After scouring the internet in search for the best strategies and techniques on successfully trading currencies, we came across Giuseppe De Marco.

Mr. De Marco worked with the prestigious Aflrio Bardolla Training Group for 10 years and transformed his first real money account from €2500 into €19,926 "demo trading."

After seeing success with his first trade, he did it a second, third and forth time. Using his secret strategies, he was able to triple his investments over the next few years.

Giuseppe continued to test, tweak and improve his techniques for over a decade before finally teaching other hungry beginners his strategies.

With more than 20,000 happy students helped, he's by far one of the most sought after authorities on trading currencies, profitably.

Mr. De Marco has helped turn broke, lazy traders, into *profitable,* lazy traders.

You see, this expert discovered, trading is all about having the *right* knowledge. In fact, he's so confident that his students will see results (even if they never have before), that he has a 3X Money Back Guarantee.

This is totally unheard of in the financial world.

<Insert Name> claims he can turn anyone who is *willing to learn* his strategies into a success.

He believes this so strongly that if you don't make back at all the money you invest to learn his secret strategies within one year, he will give you all your money back.

On top of that, Mr. <lastname> boasts that he will also reach into his own wallet and pay you twice more just for "wasting your time."

As an expert journalist, I took it upon myself to see what all the hype was about.

I was able to get a "sneak-peak" behind the curtains of Giuseppe's new course called: <course name>.

It is one of the most comprehensive courses on trading currencies I've ever seen. It is also one of the *easiest* to understand. Mr. De Marco doesn't like all the over-complicated advice given out to traders just starting out.

He says… "all that complex jargon cripples a beginner before they even start, you want beginners to start earning money right away, not suffer from learning outdated theory."

Here is some of what you'll discover in the <COURSE NAME> course:

- What's the currency trading market all about and how does it work?
- How is the currency market different from the stock market, futures markets and others?
- What's the role of the brokers, their interests and why do you need them?
- What are you responsibilities as an investor?
- How to get started, quickly
- And much more

You can access this course for yourself clicking the button below:

<Insert Button>

~ SAMPLE 2 ~

How A *Laid Back* House Wife Was Able To Defend Her House

Without A Guard Dog, Alarm System Or An Over-Priced Security Gate

By {Add Customer's Name}

Last summer, I was enjoying an outdoor BBQ with a couple of my best friends.

The couple who owned the house, was my closest friends which were the type to own 3 German shepherds, the best alarm system money could buy and loaded to the brim with weapons.

We instantly clicked after meeting just a few years ago through work and my husband, immediately loved them, too.

He became even more of a "gun" man, buying them like candy and we now have about 11 or more.

At first I was scared to use them and little unsure about them being in the house.

But, this quickly changed after I shot the AK-74 and the AR-15, which are now my FAVORITES.

If you're looking for a gun with little, to no recoil, then these are the perfect fit for you.

They've even been reported as some of the BEST guns for women and easiest to handle under pressure, which I can say from experience.

Anyways time flew by while chatting, laughing and eating, now it's was time to go.

They offered to walk us to the car...chatting the whole way, stepping outside the house, I noticed (again) the NEW sign outside their front door.

It was a "WARNING: German Shepherds Live Here" sign.

After knowing, everything about them and what they *carry* with them, I was curious why they needed a sign.

What more could a sign do, which their guns or dogs couldn't do?

I was over loaded with curiosity and had to ask them about it.

Why "WARN" them?

Frankly, we all know it doesn't take a genius to rob someone.

But it does takes a small, specific set of skills (which anyone could learn by using Youtube these days).

Burglars will scope out a neighborhood and choose the best looking house.

This means, they are only choosing by what they "think" is inside your house.

Before you start to worry, this doesn't mean you need to move into the ugliest house on the block to safe your family and belongings.

It's easy to spook someone who's trying to break into your house, without any additional home security.

You see, what they're doing is complexly illegal and this causes them to keep looking behind them through the whole process.

Once, they're spooked by something, they'll bolt and give up on robbing you.

Whether it's a dog barking or the blaring house alarm going off...they won't make it far past the door.

But what if you could stop them BEFORE they mess up your door locks, break down your door or worse, trash your house?

Yes, this is possible!

You see, this is where the warning sign comes into play.

Before, seeing the dogs, hearing the barks or setting off the alarm...they'll see the sign which shows them the exact animal who will be chasing them down the driveway while taking a chunk out of their thighs.

What if you don't have a dog?

The thing is, I don't have any dogs.

But, my household does own a small arsenal of weapons.

(Remember, my husband is a huge "gun" man and loaded up on them.)

So, I started my search for something to help a "gun owner" without dogs.

Seriously, there has to be a sign for this right?

Well, it only took close to 15 minutes to find exactly what I was looking for.

This sign shows the world, my house is protect by the "2nd Amendment" and they will see SEVERE consequences for stepping into our house *uninvited.*

What better place to put a warning sign than at the front door, as a welcome matt.

You see, this has come in handy on more than one occasion.

And if you're a proud gun owner (who wants to defend your house, while saving a little ammo) then you definitely want to give this bad boy a try.

I knew this was unbeatable when...

On the Thursday, two weeks after placing my door matt out, my neighbor came over.

She looked concerned, worried and down right, frazzled.

So, I invited her in for some tea and to see if she wanted to talk about it.

This is where she spilled her guts, telling me about seeing a man, walking around our house looking through the windows.

Or at least trying to, because I've made it almost impossible to get into any window due to the thick *thorny* bushes around each one. Neat trick, right?

She went on to say, this man was fidgeting with our door trying to get in and she was just about to call the police.

But, all of a sudden the man froze while looking down then darted off toward the street like his feet were on fire.

She had never seen anything like it and wanted to tell me right away.

"I didn't understand why he ran off until I came to knock on your day and saw your welcome mat," she said.

Then she asked me where I got it so she can get one for herself and her daughters who moved out.

You see, this mat saved my life and my house many times now.

Even when you don't even know it.

The best part is, it doesn't take a dog or more work on your part…it will effortlessly guard your house for you.

Proclaiming to the WORLD, you're a proud owner of a gun and NOT afraid to use it.

Really soon, you'll be having ALL the robber shaking in their booties and avoiding your WHOLE neighborhood.

Click here to get your door mat.

~ SAMPLE 3 ~

Diabetes-Free in Just 14 Days... Revolutionary Secret or Internet Scam?

One doctor claims to be able to eradicate Type 2 Diabetes quickly, effectively, and without injections of medications

Patricia Grey
Freelance Health Writer

I arrived at the Starbucks at the appointed time. There was a good looking man in what appeared his 50's waiting for me. His style sense, watch and general ease about life suggested a level of financial and professional success that one would expect from a successful Doctor.

"Hello, my name is Patricia" I said with a cold professional tone. Having looked into hundreds of these "Miracle Solutions," I suspected this man was just another huckster making a buck hustling desperate and sick people out of their money.

Through a large smile he said, "Hi Patricia, I'm David. It's a pleasure."

"Dr Pearson, I appreciate you meeting with me. I am interested in your diabetes program. You claim people can be diabetes free in just 14 days?"

"OK then, right down to business," he chuckled. David went on to explain how after seeing an important woman in his youth die a slow and painful death from diabetes, he dedicated himself to finding the true cause of diabetes and discovering how to eliminate it forever.

"Patricia, the prevalence of diabetes has grown from .93% in 1958 to 7.4% in 2015 . That means the average American is 800% more likely to have diabetes today than he was in 1958. That's outrageous!"

"Medical science has truly dropped the ball on diabetes. Why is there no substantial improvements in the treatment of diabetics in the last 57 years? We've eliminated polio. Even smallpox is eradicated. The expected lifespan of a 20 year old who is diagnosed with Aids is 73 years old. But with diabetes, no real paradigm shift in treatment since the 50's."

"Now I want you to think about something, the average lifespan of an American is 78.7 years. A 50 year old diagnosed with diabetes can expect to have his or her life shortened by 8.5 years . That means the 50 year old is likely to die just as he or she hits 70 years old."

\<Insert Direct-Response Banner\>

"From a strictly lifespan point of view, you're better off being a 20 year old with AIDS than being a 50 year old with a diabetes diagnosis. There's something **really** wrong there!"

"And by the way, please call me David."

I didn't expect to hear such a candid and well documented response. I was instantly more interested in what David was saying.

I was curious. I was interested, and I was successfully disarmed.

David went on to explain exactly how he discovered this "miracle" and why he's risking lawsuits and even professional censure to bring this information to the public.

"Patricia, the entrenched powers are so terrified of losing their billions in yearly sales to diabetics, my license to practice is even in jeopardy. But I don't care. Every time, I think about stopping I think about my friend and how she died a slow painful death right in front of my eyes. What if this revelation had been around to help here?" David chokes out with tears in his eyes.

Talking about her clearly still makes him emotional all these years later.
What David was saying seemed reasonable. And if he was right, it made sense why people claimed they eliminated their diabetes in just days.

Interestingly, there's no dangerous drugs, no injections, and you don't even need a prescription. Still, David suggests you talk with your doctor before you do anything.

David showed me some letters from folks who recovered from their diabetes.

<Testimonial>
<Testimonial>
<Testimonial>

But what sealed it for me were David's parting words.

"Patricia, I can see you're skeptical, and I know there are a lot of dishonest people taking advantage of sick and scared people, so I don't blame you. But think about this, I didn't tell anyone about this program until spending years of research and my own money to discover this amazing program and prove it works."

"I could have easily just quietly treated people in my clinic and never put myself in harms way. But this secret belongs to everyone. It's coming through me and my team, but it's not ours...and I need to share it with the world, no matter what the personal cost is to me."

For the first time, I believe I have found a "Miracle Solution" peddler who isn't a "Miracle Solution" peddler. He's a guy who uncovered an amazing secret about one of the nation's most deadly diseases...and he wants share it with the world.

And it's clear to me that's exactly what he's doing.

EDITOR'S NOTE: After reviewing hundreds of "Miracle Solution" quacks, Dr David Pearson is the only person I trust to show my readers how they may be able to quickly and easily eliminate diabetes in just days. There's no drugs, no injections, and you don't even need a prescription. (check with your doctor before starting any medical treatment.) While it is available, Dr Pearson has created a presentation for diabetics and their loved ones. Between civil law suits and professional and legal threats, the presentation could come down at any moment. If you are diabetic or someone you love is, click here and watch the presentation for some eye opening insight to the real cause of diabetes and what can be done to help those suffering from the disease.]

I WOULD MAKE THE ENTIRE EDITOR'S NOTE A CLICKABLE IMAGE

~ SAMPLE 4 ~

Scientific Study Reveals Miracle Joint Supplement For Dogs Guaranteed To Relieve Your Dog's Pain And Keep Them Healthy For Years To Come...
Or You Pay NOTHING!

Veterinarians From Around The World Are SHOCKED By This Amazing Discovery...

By: P.K. Marie

DATELINE - Do you have a dog that's having terrible joint pain? Pain you wish you could take away?

As an investigative reporter, I knew this incredible discovery could be the solution millions of dog owners have secretly been waiting for. I have a Sussex Spaniel/Chocolate Lab mix, named Chucky. He is the sweetest dog who ever lived and who ever will live (although admittedly, I am biased).

He just turned twelve this year, and I have been afraid he may develop the notorious Lab hip problems, so I have always kept a close eye on him.

About 3 months ago, Chucky started having problems with stairs. When we would go upstairs to bed, Chucky would pace back and forth, hesitate at the bottom of the steps and whine before finally coming up the stairs; he was in pain.

It broke my heart. Some nights, he stayed downstairs, and I know he didn't like being away from us. He also started sleeping on the bathroom tile during the day, I think the cold felt good on his sore joints.

After about a month of this behavior, I realized it was not just a pulled muscle or something temporary, so I started researching supplements.

I discovered that there are many diseases that affect the joints of dogs, so many, in fact, that there are 10 major classifications. Joint diseases occur as a result of:

1. Ligament, tendon, or muscle disease
2. Fractures involving the joint
3. Developmental disorders, i.e. hip dysplasia, elbow dysplasia, osteochondritis dissecans, Legg-Perthes disease
4. Congenital disorders
5. Dietary and hormonal disease such as hyperparathyroidism, obesity
6. Metabolic disorders
7. Cancer
8. Degenerative joint disease (osteoarthritis)
9. Inflammatory joint disease such as Lyme disease and rheumatoid arthritis

10. Degenerative spinal joint disease

After weeks of intense research I stumbled upon Candid Science's Joint Health for dogs supplement.

How It Works

The directions say to give the dog 2 pills a day for the first month, and then go down to 1 pill a day after that as a maintenance dose. That means this one bottle will last Chucky 2 months after the initial treatment, which is very convenient for us and our wallets (although I would gladly spend any amount of money to make my Big Brown Boy feel better). I'm sure you can relate.

It has been 3 and a half weeks since starting this supplement. Chucky is a whole new dog. He is active, jumping up and down, and even wrestling with Charlie, his 5 year-old German Shepherd brother.

I can actually see it in Chucky's face that he feels better. He is happier. He has a sparkle in his eye that you usually see in much younger dogs.

My Big Brown Boy has become my Big Brown Bouncing Boy, and I am so happy that he is probably going to be feeling better a lot further into old age than I previously thought possible, all because of this supplement that has absolutely changed his (and our) lives.

Now, Chucky goes up the stairs for bed with ease, and we are confident that his golden years will have a much better quality of life.

On top of that, one of the main ingredients in this miraculous supplement is glucosamine. After further investigation, a 2007 study published in The Veterinary Journal concluded that dogs treated with glucosamine showed less pain and more mobility after 70 days of treatment.

I couldn't believe the amazing results Chucky was experiencing so I set out to find other customers of the product to see if they noticed similar improvements with their dogs.

Here's what dog owners just like you and I are saying:

<Insert Testimonial>
<Insert Testimonial>
<Insert Testimonial>

Getting Started Is Easy

This is the official nation-wide release of Candid Science's Joint Supplement in the United States. And so, the company is offering a special RISK-FREE Trial to any dog owner who calls within the next 48 hours.

An order Hotline has been set up for local readers to call. This gives everyone an equal chance to try Candid Science's Joint Supplement .

Starting at 7:00 A.M. today, the **FREE** trial offer will be available for 48 hours. All you have to do is call **TOLL-FREE 1-800-###-####** right now. Then provide the operator with the special RISK-FREE trial approval code: **XXXX**. The company will do the rest.

Important: Due to Candid Science's recent media exposure, phone lines are often busy. If you call and do not immediately get through, please be patient and call back.

~ SAMPLE 5 ~

Shopify Store Owner? Then, Continue Reading...

EXPOSED: How You're Selling Yourself SHORT With Shopify...

If you're spending all your time invested in shopify, you probably haven't had the chance to see this.

Listen, we both know, there's plenty of people becoming HUGE successes, due to Shopify.

But what the experts don't mention is, all the hard work it takes to make it to the top.

Now, I know what you're thinking,

"No pain, no gain..."

Well, there's a difference between - putting in effort and working your butt off.

And personally, I know you can easily make money *without* working your butt off for it.

However, with Shopify you may be spending too much time doing labor intensive work instead of pushing more traffic and making more sales.

It's much harder to pick up and go, let's say for a vacation, if you have to be tied down due to physical products.

And if you're using shopify, it's very likely, you're selling physical products.

The worst part is, having to fork over more of your money to pay for the product in the first place.

But, I'm going to let you in on a secret. Think you can handle keeping it to yourself?

Frankly, you can share this one but keep it to your close friends and family - we don't want to the whole world knowing our secret.

You see, an easier way to make money online, build a large email list and create a bond of loyalty with your customers is with a sales funnel.

More importantly, by using ***Clickfunnels.***

In fact, if you're not using Clickfunnels, you could be leaving thousands, if not millions of dollars on the table.

You could literally be making millions right now, **without shipping a product** or seeing a customer face to face.

It's AMAZING! And super easy to work with.

But before I overwhelm you with all this awesome information and overload your brain, here's a quick breakdown for you...

What Is A Sales Funnel And How Can It Help You Take Your Business To The Next Level...

A sales funnel is a process where you can pluck a cold lead off the net, warm them up with valuable/beneficial information and build a rapport before asking for the sale. This increases your "purchase" conversions and decrease your "refund" rates.

This process helps you take a prospect from a free giveaway, to a $9.97 product, to a $225 product and even upsell them to a $7,500 product/service. (But more on this later)

I'm going to walk you through a basic sales funnel, talk about which products have been successful, and show you some of the more elegant funnels for the BIGGER ticket products.

When Do You Want To Use A Sales Funnel?

- Lead Generation - When you're looking to build an email list
- Product Sales - You can encourage your customers to tack on multiple products with upsell pages
- Event Promotion - Introduce them to your upcoming seminar and compel them to register before they seats are all taken

- Webinar Launch - Similar to event promotion, yet you can set this one to auto-pilot and all you need is a laptop and wi-fi
- Membership Site - Great way to set up a recurring income stream and provide value on a long-term basis
- And More!!

What Does A Prospect Go Through & What Does A Basic Funnel Look Like?

Your audience starts out as a "cold prospect" and needs to be "attracted" into your funnel, meaning you need to get in front and them and grab their attention.

You can do this with a banner ad, facebook ad, google ads, etc.

Once you have their attention, you want to "warm" them up to you. This is where you want to introduce your audience to something they can use or is extremely beneficial to their life at the current moment.

It's better to give this to them for free, in exchange for their contact info (name, email, phone number, etc).

Now, they've transformed from a "cold prospect" into a warm lead.

After they've had the chance to warm up to you, they like what you're putting out and convinced you can help make life better for them...you'll want to pitch them on a product.

Using a sales page, you can introduce them to the product, build trust and show them you're an expert - all without seeing them face-to-face.

By the time they reach the bottom of the page, they're dying to order their very own [INSERT YOUR PRODUCT].

So, they'll click over to your checkout page where they can put in their payment information, confirm they want the order and actually, purchase your product.

Then, they'll be directed to your Thank You page, where you can congratulate them on their purchase, give them a direct download link/button and drive them to join your facebook group or follow you on social media.

It's simple, to the point and does ALL of the work for you.

It looks a little like this:

Ad ⇒ Opt-In Page ⇒ Sales Page ⇒ Check Out ⇒ Thank You Page
[INSERT "Clickable" EXAMPLES OF FUNNEL]

Which Products Have Been Extremely Successful?

- Digital Products (Great for Freebie Giveaway or Small Baller Products):
    1. eBook
    2. Templates

3. Audio Content
  4. Video Courses
  5. Case Studies with Tutorials
  6. Training Webinar
  7. Newsletter
  8. Sample Products
  9. Reports
- Physical Products:
  1. Apparel
  2. Accessories
  3. Gadgets
  4. Books
  5. CDs
  6. Newsletters
- Recurring Products:
  1. Monthly Membership
  2. Webinars
  3. Monthly Box Subscriptions

What MORE Can You Do With ClickFunnels...

1. Upsells
[INSERT "Clickable" PICTURE OF FUNNEL]
2. Event Promotion
[INSERT "Clickable" PICTURE OF FUNNEL]
3. Webinar
[INSERT "Clickable" PICTURE OF FUNNEL]
4. Membership
[INSERT "Clickable" PICTURE OF FUNNEL]
5. Reader's Choice

[INSERT BANNER]

Look, we both know this is way more than enough info to help you make a decision...

...so, you have two choices.

You could ignore what you've just seen - continue down the path you're on, only making money through shopify with physical products, more work and expensive overhead costs (practically giving a HUGE chunk of your profits away)....

...or you can take advantage of what I've shown you, choose which template works best for you, set your funnel up to run sales on autopilot, and put more of the profits into your account and (& not the factory's pocket).

Look, you already know you can be successful with physical products. Imagine what you can do when you don't have to spend time shipping, managing dropshippers, or running to the post office.

Could you benefit from taking a larger percentage of your sales home, as *profit?*

Then, I think you're ready to dive in and see what Clickfunnels can really do for you.

The best part is, you can sign up for a 14 day trial completely FREE, to give you an insider's look and feel, without investing upfront.

If you hurry, you'll get instant access to the **sales funnel templates** and have a funnel created before the end of the day.

You basically, type in your content where necessary and the page is practically designed for you.

You'll be seeing results in no time!

Button:
Yes, I Want To Join!
(And Build My First Sales Funnel)

~ SAMPLE 6 ~

Exposed! The #1 Skin Care Secret Hollywood Starlets Use To Stay Young Through Their 40s, 50s, 60s and Beyond!

<Insert Before and After Pics>

DATELINE- Have you ever wondered how Hollywood celebrities seem to look young no matter how old they are?

Most people do… and most credit this phenomenon to plastic surgery and face lifts.

It's true, Hollywood is riddled with surgery-happy celebrities, excited for the next "tummy-tuck" or "nose-job" breakthrough.

But that's not everyone.

In fact, we've scoured the internet in search of inside information regarding the rumors of some skin-care rejuvenation secret celebrities are hoarding to themselves.

And we <u>found it!</u>

<Insert Before and After Pics>

The Skin Care Secret Hollywood Celebs Hoard For Themselves

This secret has been kept under wraps for some time and is only now starting to gain media exposure and publicity.

It's been credited to giving numerous Hollywood starlets "ageless skin."

Consumers have reported spending thousands of dollars on ineffective skin creams and treatments and up until now... it seemed as if there was no hope for *everyday* people to have access to these miraculous skin secrets.

<Insert Before and After Pics>
How To Look 15 Years Younger!

Investigative journalists have spilled the beans on the primary ingredient for this celebrity skin care secret.

It's called Diatomaceous Earth.

This is a naturally-formed grainy mineral rock which comes from the remains of diatoms.

You see, diatoms are over 30 million years old and are formed from the cementation of tiny, algae-like plant remains into the earth's surface.

These clay-like, chalky remains are known as diatomaceous earth.

Since diatomaceous earth is extremely potent, it's often used as a facial exfoliator.

The process of exfoliation is important in skin care and helps remove dead skin cells that give the appearance of tired, worn-out skin.

The best part is, after using this, consumers are claiming that their skin looks 15... even 20 years younger!

<Insert Before and After Pics>
Scientifically Formulated To Work...

After this discovery was made, medical companies invested in the formulation of a potent (and safe) product called Gaia Gala.

The #1 ingredient is Diatomaceous Earth and it's been creating success stories almost daily.

Gaia Gala is specifically formulated to naturally erase wrinkles and fine lines on a cellular level... taking decades off your skin and making you look years younger!

In fact, they're so confident you'll see results, Gaia Gala also offers a full money-back guarantee to prove it!

It's one of the rare discoveries consistently being used by celebrities to ensure that their skin looks like a million-dollars for every event.

<Insert Before and After Pics>

How To Use Gaia Gala

Using Gaia Gala is incredible easy and simple.

> **Step 1** – Cleanse your face and pat it dry
> **Step 2** – Apply Gaia Gala Skin Smoother evenly over your face and neck
> **Step 3** – Watch as your wrinkles and signs of aging begin to disappear

Listen, you try to keep your body healthy and nourished, right?

So, why not take care of your skin also?

See, your face is constantly exposed to harsh elements, including sun, dirt, wind and pollution.

That means, your skin needs protection and gentle care to undo *years* of damage and finally reveal your youthful glow.

Gaia Gala works to reverse signs of aging like wrinkles, fine lines, age spots and dullness.

On top of that, unlike other, more diluted brands, it also treats other unpleasant skin conditions.

If you're even slightly interested in reversing your skins aging process, Gaia Gala is the all in one clinical quality treatment that does more for less.

Plus, your skin care investment is completely protected with Gaia Gala's 100% money-back guarantee which covers you for a full 30 days.

That means, if for some reason you don't like Gaia Gala Skin Smoother you can get a full refund within 30 days.

Margaret's Story...

"I didn't think using a natural product would have the same effect as the expensive stuff
I was getting from my dermatologist, but my sister in law was raving about Gaia Gala so I ordered some for myself.

After a month I honestly look 15 years younger - I'm officially a believer."
- Margaret, 51, Massachusetts

<Insert Before And After Pics>
Will This Work For You?

There are plenty of skincare gimmicks out there, and frankly, most of them are incredibly expensive.

And with so many options, it's only natural for you to be skeptical about the results.

Gaia Gala is extremely affordable for anyone and has been proven to work over and over again.

There's no way Gaia Gala could offer a 30-day money back guarantee if this *didn't* work.

They would go out of business because of all the refunds.

However, since we don't want to make any outlandish promises, we simply want to challenge you to do what has been recommended by thousands of others just like you:

Try Gaia Gala Skin Smoother for 30-Days RISK-FREE!

If it's worked for all these other people, chances are high, that you'll see incredible results as well.

For your convenience, we have provided the link to try Gaia Gala for yourself.
Button: <Yes I Want To Try Gaia Gala For 30 Days RISK-FREE!>

~ SAMPLE 7 ~

EXPOSED! Does Their Snoring Keep You Up At Night?
<current date>

DATELINE- Do you or your partner have a snoring problem?

Most of the time, the person snoring isn't the one who's suffering.

It's the person *next* to them... hiding under the pillow, trying desperately to drown out the snore violating their ears.

Mayo Clinic explains that snoring happens when tissues in the throat relax enough to partially block the airway and cause vibrations. You see, when you sleep, muscles in the soft palate, tongue and throat naturally relax.

Air through the mouth and nose becomes more forceful as the airways narrow, causing the snoring to get louder and louder.

On top of that, chronic nasal congestion increases snoring by making it harder for air to pass through the nose.

As you get older, the aging process gradually relaxes your throat muscles, so snoring may naturally occur later in your life.

Snoring Can Kill You!

Snoring isn't just an annoyance... it's a scary sign of what may come.

Dr. Raina Gupta[1], a neurologist and sleep medicine specialist at Advocate Illinois Masonic Medical Center in Chicago says "Anyone who snores heavily, especially if it keeps your partner awake at night, should check with their physician about having a sleep study.

Dr. Gupta continues by saying…

"The sooner you know whether or not you have sleep apnea and how severe it might be, the sooner you can be treated and avoid any possible long-term damage to your heart."

In fact, Dr. Gupta warns that "poor sleep can change the hormones in your body, which affects the way fat is stored."

When that happens he reveals that "Extra fat is stored, which can lead to an elevated risk of diabetes and heart disease."

Listen, the last thing you want to is to have someone you care about get heart disease because they didn't think there was a solution.

The good news is, there *is* a solution…and I'll reveal it in just a moment…

The Reason For Loud Snoring?

Snoring worsens when someone breathes through the mouth rather than the nose, especially with a larger soft palate. According to MedicineNet.com, snoring intensifies and gets louder if the nose is stuffed or blocked in some way.

The effects of snoring can also cause whoever is in the bed to toss and turn the entire night… making it impossible to get a good night sleep.

<Insert Direct-Response style banner>
After a long day of work, the last thing most people want to do is toss and turn the whole night.
That's why we've scoured the internet in search of a solution.
A solution that can end snoring for good.
And guess what?
We found it!

The Cure To Snoring?

After searching high and low, we stumbled across SnoreGuardian.

They guarantee results.

In fact, they go as far as to say that if you use SnoreGuardian, annoying and chronic snoring will stop ***permanently***.

At first, we were a little skeptical about whether or not something like this would actually work.

So, we put it to the test.

One of our staff members complained that her husband never stopped snoring and it was ruining their sleep!

She told her husband to try SnoreGuardian and after the first night, they were hooked.

Her husband was a little hesitant at first, but after having a full 8 hours of uninterrupted sleep… he was sold!

Here's How It Works…

SnoreGuardian supports your jaw, holds it forward and opens the airway. This stops snoring and helps increase oxygen levels. When this happens, you'll have improved REM sleep, lower blood pressure and even diminish day time fatigue.

The best part is, it's portable so you can take it on your vacations or when traveling. It's light weight, easy to wear and extremely comfortable.

Diane's Story...

Diane is 50 years old and lives in Kansas. She wrote in saying this about her experience with SnoreGuardian:

"My husband has snored for years which has resulted in us having to sleep in separate bedrooms. It was hard on our marriage and we tried just about everything to fix the problem.

I saw a great review of SnoreGuardian online so I decided to buy one on a whim because it was so affordable. It has significantly reduced his snoring to the point where we can share a bed again! I am so pleased, thank you for this great product!"

That's incredible isn't it?

SnoreGuardian literally saved her marriage and stopped her husband's unbearable snoring.

Get Yours FREE?

As a service to our readers, we've contacted SnoreGuardian and asked if they can give you a special deal on this amazing product.

They agreed!

For a limited time, you're can test-drive SnoreGuardian for a full 30-days RISK-FREE!

On top of that, you'll also get a BONUS SnoreGuardian absolutely **FREE** when you click here now.

You see, SnoreGuardian is guaranteed to work.

That means, if there's ever a reason you're unhappy with your SnoreGuardian, simply send it back within 30 Days for a full refund!

That makes this incredible offer totally **RISK-FREE!**

What could be more fair?

Don't spend another night suffering – get SnoreGuardian today by clicking the button below.

Button <Next Page>

~ SAMPLE 8 ~

The Death Of Shopify?

If you own a Shopify store… READ THIS!

Like most folks, you've probably noticed that Shopify is becoming more and more popular. And it's for good reason.

See, it's allowed people to go from zero to hero in a very short amount of time. The thing is… there's a dark side to Shopify you never know about… until you're in too deep.

When you own a Shopify store, chances are good that you also sell physical products.

Now, with physical products, you need to make sure your systems and processes are dialed in… especially when you scale.

Otherwise, you'll be dealing with refunds, complaints, shut down merchant accounts and more.

And that's never fun.
<Insert Banner>
Listen, I love Shopify.

I own a store myself and even coach a lot of my clients on how to optimize their stores for maximum conversions.

But there's an easier, simpler and more profitable way to earn a stable income online.

I'm talking about selling with *funnels*.

You see, when you use funnels to sell your products, you can easily lead your prospects down a proven pathway for long term customer sustainability.

Even Shopify agrees! This was quoted from their website:

"Ecommerce stores should be leveraging the power of sales funnels to turn cold traffic into new customers through innovative free+shipping offers that lead into a value ladder of higher-priced products."

The #1 way to leverage the power of sales funnels is by using a proven-to-convert funnel builder called ClickFunnels. ClickFunnels makes creating million-dollar funnels simple and easy.

In fact, you can create your funnel in less than an hour and start driving targeted traffic towards it. You can get a FREE 14-Day trial of ClickFunnels by clicking the button below

<Yes! I Want ClickFunnels For FREE!>

Section 18: What's next?

When your reader becomes a subscriber, you now have their personal contact information.

What are you going to do with it?

Well, maybe you want to deliver your lead magnet…

…or you want to upsell them to a larger product/service.

Either way, you'll want to use email marketing to pull this act off.

In these next chapters, you'll discover the difference between a promotional email and an affiliate email.

Plus, I'll show you exactly how to write these emails yourself.

This way, you'll have everything from your Facebook ad to your advertorial and have your email marketing, all planned out.

Turn the page to get a peak at my 10 Methods For Ensuring Your Email Body Copy Is NOT Boring (& Encourages Them To Act Right Away)!

Chapter 35 - Email marketing

Emails are very similar to Facebook ads - if your subject line doesn't draw attention and captivate your audience - they won't click through to open your email.

In this case, your subject line is more important than a Facebook Ad headline.

Why?

Simple, if your audience reads your headline, they may not like it, but they'll probably glance at the text and read through it for a second.

If your subject line doesn't capture their eye, then they won't even open the email.

So, the only thing they'll see is your subject line and NOTHING more.

Remember back to when you were looking through your inbox last…

How many "unread" emails did you have?

Did you open each and every one of them?

You see, most often than not, your audience will scan through their email box filled with 127 emails and only look for the ones that stand out.

When you have a list of subject lines to look at, what helps one subject line stand out more than another one?

Well, I'm about to reveal a few simple techniques you can use to get your emails opened and increase your click through rates as well!

Let's start with your subject line and what you can do to make them POP.

You want them to be so POWERFUL, your audience has no other option but to click on it and open it up.

6 Techniques To Use For Writing Successful Subject Lines:

1. Keep it short - or the email provider may cut off some words if they don't fit
2. Make it personal - use their name when you can, make it resonate
3. Don't "tell" them - give them a taste but not the whole candy bar
4. Show them an impressive benefit - how will it make a difference
5. Give it a Call To Action - sometimes it easier just to tell them what you want them to do

6. And create a sense of urgency - quick, before we leave….

10 Methods For Ensuring Your Email Body Copy Is NOT Boring (& Encourages Them To Act Now):

1. Two sentences before the introduction - most email providers will show the first two sentences along with the subject line, so include a couple lines before your introduction
2. Use compelling & resonating questions - the best type are the ones that elicit a "Yes!" answer from them, identifying with something they're currently thinking
3. Break up your sentences - don't put more than 3 sentences in the same paragraph, if your copy is bulky it's harder to read and repels their attention
4. Offer valuable tips - you could give them one major tip or multiple small tips, but they need to feel like you're helping them without asking for anything in return
5. Use stories to tag them along - in your longer emails, you can use a story to tie in your product with their lives at the moment
6. Make them feel like you understand - you want them to feel like you understand where they're coming from, like you've been through something similar

7. Don't ALWAYS sell something - use the 80/20 rule and only pitch after delivering a ton of value, for every 3 value emails, send a pitch email
8. Introduce your offer as a *possible* solution - down shove your offer down their throats, make it subtle and they'll feel like they made the decision on their own
9. Don't forget your P.S. - this is the perfect place to ask for feedback, get your readers to connect on Facebook, grow your group, or make another subtle offer
10. Always make sure your message flows smoothly - your story, questions and offer all must be relevant to each other - do not write in a random manner

At the end of this section, you'll have plenty of example emails to look over and help you write your very own.

Enjoy!

Chapter 36 - Lead Magnet delivery

So, you have their contact information.... what are you going to say them to now?

After they've given you their information, it's time to deliver on what you promised.

You see, the best way to get your audience to hand over their personal information is by offering something in return.

And most times, this a "freebie" lead magnet like an eBook, report, study guide, etc.

The logical thing to do first would be to deliver this lead magnet and thank them for subscribing, correct?

Yes!

Now, after thanking them and showing your appreciation, you can use your emails to:

> → Deliver more value
> → Upsell them on another product/service
> → Send them to a blog site
> → Send deals, coupons, and promotions

Here's an email sequence you can follow, after they've opted-in:

Email 1: Lead Magnet Delivery
Email 2: Value/Lead Magnet Delivery
Email 3: Value
Email 4: Value/Subtle Offer
Email 5: Offer
Email 6: Value
Email 7: Value/Subtle Offer

You want to give your audience at least two chances to download their lead magnet.

This will re-establish that you don't want them to miss it and gives you an opportunity to email them without spamming them.

When you're delivering value, you seem more like an article and giving your audience more than taking from them.

This sequence follows the 80/20 rule.

This means it delivers 80% value with only 20% pitch.

You want to your audience to over value your advice and information.
It will help keep them on the edge of their seats waiting for your next email.

If you're always delivering awesome information, then they'll want to continue reading your emails.

And you won't end up in the spam folder.

Once you have their attention, and they see you so highly, then you can start to subtly pitch them.

You've gained their trust even more with the valuable information you've given them, now is the perfect time to subtly push them towards something you think could benefit them.

A good transition sentence is,

"Since, you've been reading my emails and shown some interest in my _____... I figured you would also love this, as well! It's exactly what we've talking about, and it's already been proven to work. Give it a try."

Then you can either cut it there if you want it short and simple.

Or you can write it as a long form email, and include more to it with a story and some awesome benefits to tie it all together.

I've personally seen some great results from both short form and long form, it all depends on your audience and what they're looking for from you.

I would test both and see which is best for your specific list.

You may find it's the exact opposite of what you're thinking.

It's happened so many times, I'm not surprised anymore and can pinpoint which one it will be before testing.

However, I still test it out to make sure. The internet world is changing so often, and it's all because of the demand of consumers.

So, we can safely assume, the consumers are changing just as frequently – they just might not talk about it as much.

Keep this in mind, and continue testing what works best for your audience.

Chapter 37- Abandoned Cart Emails

How much are you leaving on the table?

I'm talking about money here...sales and orders you're leaving out.

You know, like when your prospects make it ALL the way to your cart but don't buy from you.

They were sold on your product/service and something distracted them from taking the last step.

These are the perfect people to follow up with.

You know for a fact, they want what you're selling.

So, now you just need to find out what made them click away at the last second and how you can get them to come back for another chance at getting your product/service.

This is a whole different type of sequence and is meant to ONLY go out to those who have made it all the way to your cart but didn't buy from you.

Why?

Simple, if someone has already seen your pitch and been through your funnel, they don't want to see it all over again.

You can spark their memory but taking them through the multiple steps of your funnel will result in you losing them along the way.

In fact, your "abandoned cart" emails tend to link straight to the cart or to a one-time offer page.

The one-time offer page tends to pull a little better, especially if you're giving a discount on the product/service they were interested in.

Contrary to popular belief, being completely honest is the best way to go.

For example, you can say something like,

"I saw you made it all the way to the cart, but for some insane reason you didn't buy…

…and I was just wondering, after all the raving reviews I'm getting about it, why you wouldn't want it as well."

This is completely honest and makes them feel a little terrible about not taking action already.
It pulls on their heartstrings, especially if you've already established a bond or connection with them.

Nobody wants to let their friends down or feel like they're being a bad friend…so, this is your advantage.

Look over the email samples I've provided and make sure you keep this in mind when you're creating your own "abandoned" cart emails.

Chapter 38 - Promo Emails

Don't forget to mix your email sequence or campaign up with a little more value than promotion.

However, when you do write a promotional email, you'll want to get the message across and convert your audience into sales.

So, here's my 4 Step Formula For Writing Promotional Emails:

- ✓ **Step 1:** Open with a story and depending on what the purpose is of the email, you can tell open looped stories that leave cliff hangers *(works well if you're writing a sequence, you can use it to get people to "stay tuned" to the next email coming)*

- ✓ **Step 2:** Tie in how the lesson of the story *can solve their problem, relate to them, and entertain them*

- ✓ **Step 3:** Close out with a call to action and either appreciation for them reading your message or a promise that what they see on the next page will be *worth their time*

- ✓ **Step 4:** After your signature, always have at least 1 P.S. recapping a lesson and giving them another CTA with link to click *(usually anchor text link like, "click on this link right now")*

This is very similar to how you write an advertorial, a sales letter, and even a webinar.

You'll see this is the fundamentals to most pieces of copy.

If you can get this formula down pat, you can sell just about ANYTHING.

And you'll have loyal customers for life who keep coming back for more & more!

~ Email Sequence 1 ~

Emails 1, 2, 3 – To take them from "financial freedom" to Forex - AFTER opting in to the "colder" bribe

SL 1: <Firstname>, here's your Gift!

SL 2: Hey <Firstname>, did you receive your gift, yet?

Hey <Firstname>,

Here's the download link for your "Insert Name Of Bribe"

CLICK HERE TO DOWNLOAD >>>

My goal is for you to master currency trading so you can make millions, reach financial freedom and tap in to your true potential.

"Insert Name Of Bribe" gives you the tools necessary for you to succeed.

I've made it my mission, to show you how to succeed with "currency" trading.

Most people fall flat on their face… using the strategies I'll reveal to you, I *rarely* lose money.

My suggestion is to first go through the "Insert Name Of Bribe" from beginning to end.

Now at first, you may stop short when you see how much information we're giving you.

But don't worry.

This happens to almost everyone.

So, when you keep reading, you'll pleasantly discover that it's much easier to take in and has been broken down into smaller sections to make it easy to soak in.

Sooner or later though, you'll blow right past the terminology and master the "art of the trade."

In a few years, you'll be looking back at this day laughing.

You'll realize how simple it really was to become a success.

Anyway, I just wanted to help you on your journey.

I'll be sending you an email every now and then.

They'll be stuffed with helpful tips, techniques and strategies you can use to trade *smarter.*

Now go ahead and download <name of report> right now by clicking here.

To Your Success,

Sign

P.S. Keep an eye out for those future emails.

They'll be packed with new strategies, current stories from the news and *insider information* that may affect the markets (plus your profits).

Email 2:

SL 1: Is the office too loud today? I thought I would turn…

SL 2: Looking for a quieter place to work? I know this spot over by the…

Sitting on my couch, laptop on, and besides the music in the background, it's absolutely quiet.

Pretty serene, if you ask me.

And this is how I work, almost every day of the week.

You see, I don't miss the days where I would wake up to a blaring alarm, rushing around the house to complete my morning tasks before having to dash out the door to make sure I made it to work on time.

After stepping off the elevator while walking towards my office, I realized the office seemed like a war zone.

If you stepped the wrong way, you'd run into the stampede of people scrambling to get to their offices, you can hear the loud (overbearing) voices from all of your co-workers on the phone.

The only good thing was the smell of coffee coming from the break room.

I would sit at my desk for an hour each morning, while checking my emails and "to-do" lists for the day, I would speculate why I'm even there.

It's not like I was really happy to be there.

I wasn't happy at home, either. And I definitely wasn't making the money, I *dreamed* of making.

Frankly, I would be too embarrassed to even write a *letter* to my past self, at five years old, this was not what I thought I would be doing.

You see, I wanted more out of life.

I wanted to make a better future for myself and for my family.

This is definitely not what I wanted to be doing for the next 10, 15 or even for the next 5 years.

So, I went on a mission to find every possible way to make money without a job, without a "boss" and you'd be amazed at what I've found.

What if I told you, you can make a $1,000 with only $250 to begin with?

In fact, you can make this money with less work than your boss is demanding, these days.

Seriously, I've been in the "trade" world for about 10 years.

In that time, I've pinpointed exactly which countries to invest with, market changes, and how to make sure your accounts steadily bring in profits without draining your investments.

The best part is, I've compiled every little secret, tip and trick I've learned over the years, into <u>one course.</u>

After taking this course, you'll be able to work from anywhere and reach financial freedom in half the time... or <u>you pay nothing</u>

To Your Trade Success ,

Sign

P.S. If you don't make money after following the steps I'll show you in this course...

I promise to pay you back every penny, times 3.

===> Get The Full Scoop Here

Email 3:

SL 1: Your dollar is worthless….

SL 2: Your money doesn't matter when you travel to…

Have you ever thought about traveling to another country?

How would you pay for things?

This is why we've all set up exchange offices, where you can turn your U.S. dollars in and change them out for the currency of that particular country.

For example, when you go to Britain, their currency is called a "pound" and for a U.S. dollar you'll get .80 in pounds.

Now, this tells us our dollar is worth a little less in Britain.

But it also tells us when you have pounds, they're worth a little more and in return, will make you a profit upon exchange.

With this in mind, you can make a profit off of currency exchange without even leaving your couch.

Let me explain.

===> Get The Full Scoop Here

You can join the trading world and do all your trading online.

This means, you can invest in companies like Apple, or help invest in new start-ups overseas, maybe even the next software trend, and you can do this ALL from the comfort of your own home.

Imagine, if someone introduced you to this and you could have invested in Apple before it really went big.

You would be banking right now and consistently banking for years to come because they are a smart investment due to their techs consistently inventing the next new gadget.

But if you invest in someone like that, you would be making a profit off everyone who's carrying an Iphone, listening to music through Apple earbuds and even those walking around with the New IPad Airs.

Before you start to over think this, yes, trading can be difficult at times.

And this is why, I want to share with you, exactly how I've made millions through trading and how you can too!

If you're really serious about generating monumental profits from the comfort of your own living room, then you'll definitely want to check out my new course.

The best part is, this course if filled with step-by-step lessons showing you how to make money in the trade market.

It'll walk you through what a broker is, what an indicator is and what markets are best to invest in.

Before I give you all the spoilers, check it out for yourself, **HERE.**

To Your Trade Success,

Sign

P.S. I could keep these strategies and techniques to myself, but what for?

I've already made millions with them and now it's *your* turn.

I just want to make sure you reach millions faster and without making the same mistakes most beginners make.

===> Avoid These Common Mistakes When Trading

~ Email Sequence 2 ~

Email 1:

SL 1 - 5 Simple Steps To Unlocking Your True Potential
SL 2 - How to achieve success...

What do you picture yourself doing in 5 years?

Well, what can you do today to help you get there?

These are the types of questions, successful people ask themselves, *consistently.*

[INSERT YOUR NAME] here...

You see, if you have goals in life, the only person who is going to push you to reach them is - yourself.

Frankly, if you're unhappy with where you're at in life or mad at yourself, then you can change the scenario and turn your life around.

How can you do this?

Simple, by following in the footsteps of those who have already done it.

You don't have to do it exactly the same, but if you follow 75% of what they do, you should see an inkling of what they've experienced.

Take me for example, **I've followed in the footsteps of my dear friend, Eric Fieldman.**

He took a simple, ordinary [guy/gal] like me and turned me into a success story.

I've been able to tap into my true potential and show the world, what I'm really made of.

I went from living paycheck to paycheck, depressed, single and seriously unhappy with life…

…to enjoying life with better relationships, generate millions for myself, and finally have many reasons to smile throughout the day.

It's not hard.

If I can do it, so can you.

To give you a little taste of what I'm talking about here's a few pointers you can start with:

Step 1: Make sure to get up an hour earlier - get your day started and kick your butt into gear

Step 2: Stick to productive/profitable tasks - you don't want to waste your time, when you could be making money

Step 3: Become more self-aware - know when your emotions are getting in the way, take the opportunity to grow and always strive to be a better "you"

Step 4: Visualize what you want and what it will take to get it - write down small, everyday tasks you can do to get you closer to your end goals (don't slack off, turn your dreams into a reality)

Step 5: Motivate yourself - find what helps get your energetic, enthusiastic and ready for anything...then, continue to keep it in mind so you can tackle any obstacle thrown your way!

These aren't set routines, and they aren't going to work for everyone.

You have to want it so bad, you would do anything to make it a reality.

Are your dreams enticing enough?

Then get started, before you realize months have gone by and you're still doing the same boring thing everyday.

To Upgrading Your Life To The Next Level,
Signature

P.S. You can massively improve your life, just by making small changes in your daily routine.

If it this simple, I don't know why you would wait on taking the first step.

Get started now and let me know how things go for you.

Actually, I would LOVE to hear all about it - send me a reply message with the details.

Email 2:

SL 1 - Need a change in your life?

SL 2 - How to live life to the FULLEST...

Dropping my bags at the door and slowly walking through the house, exhausted and ready for a break.

I just spent the day switching between "hats" and it can be a little overwhelming.

You know, like wearing your "thinking" cap, except there's one for just about everything.

The most important one is the "business" hat.

And it's something I keep on at all times, now.

You see, I used to be terrible about bouncing between different businesses, trying to keep my social life separately and keeping a wall up around the things I wasn't doing at that moment.

But the "mental" wall I was keeping up would start falling apart, letting in distractions and stressing me out with thoughts from other projects.

What happens when you balance your social life, your business, your health and your relationships?

It would be like the world revolved around you, where your business is thriving with less work from you, your health is flourishing and your confidence is unbreakable.

The only problem you'll have is when your cheeks get sore from smiling so much.

I've been where you might be at and if I can come back from it, accomplishing my version of success, then you can too!

It all starts with a positive mindset, self-awareness and a little discipline to keep yourself on track.

Think you can do it?

Well, I'm pretty confident you can.

And to help you out, before throwing you to the sharks...here's a great morning routine you can adopt to help improve your life on many fronts:

1 - Write out your to-do list the night before, when you wake up the next morning - you're ready to go with a list to follow

2 - Get motivated and energized IMMEDIATELY - turn some music on, grab a cup of coffee, open up the blinds, and wake up completely (avoid the snooze button!)

3 - Eat a snack as soon as possible - kick start your metabolism and fuel your body for a great day

4 - Prioritize your list of tasks - determine which ones will take the longest and which ones need to be done first

5 - Get moving! Stretch, exercise or take a walk - this will jumpstart your brain and set you up for clearer thoughts throughout the day

Try it out, sit down tonight and start #1 and have fun with it!

To Living A Tremendous Life,
Signature

P.S. I would love to know if you've added any habits to your morning routine and which ones have made the biggest difference for you.

Send me a reply with the full details! I look forward to hearing from you.

Email 3:

SL 1 - Tired of being the victim to "bad" luck?
SL 2 - Never have a bad day again?

What is your BIG reason for doing what you do?

You see, successful people tend to have a reason in mind no matter what it is they're doing.

There's something motivating them and pushing them to take action towards their dreams.

So, you can see why this is something important to keep in mind.

[INSERT YOUR NAME] here...

Frankly, your mindset is the only thing holding you back.

You could have taken your business to the next level, improved your relationship and accomplished true happiness by now if your mindset was actually in "growth" mode.

In fact, when you're in "growth" mode - you're always looking for a way to improve your day and overall, *your life.*

Have you taken a course, a class or learned something new recently?

If you had a reason for needing new knowledge, you would be attending every class you could, right?

The thing is, if you can't pinpoint your "reason" or decide what motivates you - you'll ultimately fail and continue down the wrong path.

Stop holding yourself back.

Stop second guessing yourself.

And avoid stressing about failing…

…embrace it, learn from it and move on.

A millionaire will look at *any situation* as a time to learn and they seem to find the positive *in everything*.

However, an "average joe" will see a bad situation as a time to quit and give up.

Discover the characteristics and habits you need to adopt to become a self-made millionaire, **click this link to get the full scoop!**

==>LINK

I may not be a billionaire, but I'm happy, I've made millions, I have better relationships with people, and can finally say my life is AMAZING!

If this sounds like something you would want to do as well, then you'll definitely want to check this out...

==>LINK

It's not everyday, someone hands you the key to turning your life around.

Take this opportunity while you still can.

To Living A Tremendous Life,
Signature

P.S. Don't let this email disappear.

If you ignore it, it will hide behind all the other emails you get and ultimately be forgotten.

==>LINK

You'll never know what to do to take your life to next level and **you'll be missing out on turning your dreams into a reality.**

It's your choice, make a wise decision - I promise you're making the right one when you click this link...

==>LINK

Email 4:

SL 1 - Open this alone...
SL 2 - An investment… in yourself?

Are you ready to start investing in yourself?

I don't mean money - I'm talking about, TIME.

You may have a long list of tasks to do, but how many of those tasks are **actually meant to help improve yourself?**

The thing is, to enhance how you see yourself, how you feel about yourself and overall your entire mindset…

… you need to spend time developing your self-insight and self-esteem.

Ultimately, you'll want to pinpoint what thoughts have rubbed off on you from family members and which qualities you picked up from co-workers.

And then, figure out who you want to be, where you need to go to become this person and **what you need to do to get there.**

It won't happen overnight, and your mindset will take a little more training to hone it in.

But it's completely worth it.

You see, your actions and habits are what will create results, whether they're the results you want or not.

Here's how I saw AMAZING results:

==>LINK

It's not just about positive thinking and steering yourself away from negativity.

Your thoughts can literally *sabotage* your behavior, but your actions can sabotage your overall life.

If you make the wrong turns more often than not, your days will continue to drag you down, never allowing you a single day of success.

But lucky for you…

I've found the key to reversing these terrible side effects of having a "bad" day and I want to share them with you.

==>LINK

Make sure nobody is around to read over your shoulder or listen in to what you're about to hear.

This is for your ears and eyes ONLY!

You'll be SURPRISED by how easy it is to transform a bad day into a GREAT one and turn a poor life into a *wealthier* one.

Just click and see!

==>LINK

You'll be thanking me later for this.

To Living A Tremendous Life,
Signature

P.S. Look, you can ignore this email and move on with your life. Always looking for a way to improve your mood, health and income…

…or you could <u>click this link</u> and discover just how simple it is to make your dreams a reality.

You can improve your confidence, upgrade your income, increase your health, and enhance your future relationships all from what you're about to discover!

==>LINK

Email 5:

SL 1 - Your LAST dollar?
SL 2 - How to deal with lack of money…

Have you ever invested your last dollar into something that failed?

I have.

I spent years trying to build a business of my own, only to fail, over and over again.

I would run into issues all the time.

Trying to get my expenses to lower and my profits to increase, and sometimes, it's not as easy as they make it seem.

I was going into debt trying to make it work.

And I was running out of options.

If this sounds familiar, then you're in the right place.

I'm looking to help people just like you and me, avoid this crisis and manage a *successful* life.

And not just in business.

You see, I know more than anyone, for your business to be successful...your "outside" life must be positive and smooth sailing as well.

If not, you could be bringing in lingering emotions from the "outside" world and it could be sabotaging your chances of success.

In fact, here are just a few of the ways your day could be "ruined" and go downhill:

1 Bad hair day
2 Angry people at work
3 Deadlines coming up
4 Stressed at home
5 Not getting enough food

They might sound silly to you right now, but at one time or another these small little things have ruined your day before it has even begun.

It's not something to be ashamed about.

It happens more often than you think.

However, for your day to run smoothly and your month to be a HUGE success, you'll need to build a resolve so strong...**nothing can penetrate it.**

I'm talking building your mindset up to withstand just about anything the day will throw at you.

Bad hair day - no problem, use a little gel or hairspray and you're all good!

Deadlines coming up - no worries, take a deep breath and crank it out - you got this!

You see, your attitude and mood will impact your success, health, business, happiness and your relationships.

Discover <u>the easiest way to control your emotions</u> and overall improve your life from it.

I've been where you might be at, I dug myself out and I had help getting back to the top.

This is why I'm giving you a helping hand, to ensure you get to the top and live your dream life, with less hassles and stress than it took me.

You'll get the inside scoop on what to avoid, what is essential to your success **and what to do next to get you closer to the finish line.**

Ready to get started?

==>LINK

Just keep in mind, I'm doing this for you.

I want to see you succeed.

I don't want you to get left behind and be stuck on the outside - looking in.

This is your chance to join the club.

You can finally be a "happy camper" who has no reason to stress, no complaints about life and ready for the future brings you.

To Living A Tremendous Life,
Signature

P.S. This is literally your LAST chance to check this out.

==>LINK
I don't want to leave you behind but I also don't want to pester you or waste your time when you don't want to improve your life.

So, take this opportunity while you can - **it won't be here waiting, if you put off until later.**

==>LINK

~ Email Sequence 3 ~

Email 1:

SL 1- How to better your life and make a fortune...
SL 2- Shhh… don't tell anyone I said this...

I think it's amazing!

You know, the fact that you're actually trying to become a better person and exceed other people's expectations - it's wonderful.

I have to say it…

...you're 100% AWESOME!

Not everyone wants to reach their true potential or see what limits they can push past.

Some people are ok with settling, sticking with comfort zones and accomplishing only the bare minimum.

That's not you, right?

Well, great!

You see, I personally want to make sure you know your opportunities are endless and you accomplish anything you set your mind to.

Whether it's making a million dollars, finding the woman of your dreams or traveling the world while getting paid….it's right at your fingertips.

And to help you take the right path, you can follow this well-laid out plan of action:

==>LINK

I don't want to overwhelm you or get your too excited, but what you're about to see if going to BLOW your mind.

You'll be shocked with how easy it is to make such a massive change in your life.

I can picture it now:

You're finally happy, wearing a HUGE smile almost every second of the day, relaxing on a beach somewhere with a drink in your hand...and you set your income stream to "auto-pilot" so **you don't have to worry about making money while you relax.**

If this sounds like an amazing day to you, then you'll definitely want to check this out!

==>LINK

Don't miss out on it, it's changed my life around for good and it can do the same for you, too.

To Upgrading Your Life To The Next Level,
Signature

P.S. I would love to know how this has impacted you most. Send me a message with a couple of ways this has changed your life. I look forward to hearing from you.

Email 2:

SL 1- Is your life… boring?
SL 2- The most important email you'll ever read…

Tired of living a boring, well-maintained life?

Looking to turn your life into an adventure?

Tapping into your true potential is much like releasing a beast into the wild.

You'll experienced high levels of euphoria and happiness.

Your work performance will increase exponentially. (You may even breach the million dollar bracket…)

Your relationships will improve.

Your confidence will be unbreakable and your life will be worth enjoying for a change.

If you only live once, shouldn't be on your terms?

Then, take back control and discover what you can do when you're at your BEST.

==>LINK

It's not hard to take the first step.

You literally just have to click this link and follow along as we show you what to do to take your life to the next level.

==>LINK

You'll see what it takes to build your self-awareness, boost your self-esteem and lower your risks of falling into a whole of depression.

I want to help you manage your everyday stress and find what motivates you to turn your dreams into a reality.

To Upgrading Your Life To The Next Level,
Signature

P.S. This isn't about me.

I'm looking out for you. I want you to be able to live your dream life and live it completely on your own terms.

I thought it would be easier for you if I just showed you the way.

==>LINK

Email 3:

SL 1- How to "Go BIG!"
SL 2- Why settling is your BIGGEST enemy...

This guy's story, blew my mind.

Seriously, he started out so low and ending up a self-made millionaire.

If you're anything like me, you've thought about going BIG but didn't see the path to take you there.

You see, I was a lot like him, living in a small community, where everyone knew who you were, you went to school with the same kids every year and you can't keep a secret to save a life.

I thought I was going nowhere in life - which technically, was true at the time.

I was spending countless hours at work, with nothing to show for it but a long list of debt.

Nothing is cheap these days.

And couldn't see myself expanding anytime soon.

I would be stuck at a set income level and living paycheck to paycheck.

Frankly, this is no way to live.

And if you've made this far - you feel the same way, right?

Well, get a look at how this guy turned his life around, became a self-made millionaire and trained countless other "ordinary" people how to do it, too.

What you're about to see is going to **SHOCK** you.

But, keep in mind - this has been proven to work and is completely LEGAL to do.

I'm not trying to turn you into a criminal.

I want to make ethical money, live your dream life, make better relationships, and increase your health.

==>LINK

The only way I can do this is by showing you exactly what he showed me and if you take action, you'll be amazed with the results!

To Upgrading Your Life To The Next Level,
Signature

P.S. As silly as it sounds, You Only Live Once, and it should be spent the way you want to, right?

Discover the key to better health, an increase in business, incredible relationships and unbreakable confidence in yourself.

Avoid going down the wrong path, wasting years, feeling unhappy and stressed out. I'll show you the way!

==>LINK

Email 4: [Day 4 Email 1]

SL 1- Poor Vs Rich (which do you choose?)...
SL 2- (Urgent) It's up to you...

I've been poor.

However recently, I've become wealthier.

And I can honestly say, I would rather be upset with money than enthusiastically poor.

You see, no matter how much money I make, there's still people depending on me.

I could either - have enough money to take care of everyone **or I could make enough just to pay my own bills and absolutely nothing else.**

I couldn't take it anymore, looking at family members who were in debt and couldn't afford their house let alone groceries for next week.

It's devastating to watch people who are close to you, run their lives into the ground and be left with nothing.

But it's even worse, when you're in the same boat and you can't help them out.

You're both just sinking, with a tiny bucket to scoop the water out of your boat.

What if you could make a simple change to your daily routine and generate an increasingly amount of business, plus turn your relationships around *for good?*

Well, after seeing this - **you'll be SHOCKED with how easy it is.**

==>LINK

In fact, it's the same exact path I've taken to turn my life around, build myself into a self-made millionaire, and find the [woman/man] of my dreams.

And I can assume, since you're reading this - you want to see some of the same results I've seen.

So, take advantage while you can...

==>LINK

Today is literally your LAST chance to see this.

After this, your email will be forgotten and this link won't work anymore.

If you want to make the change in your life you need to become a self-made millionaire…

... then you'll want to click over now.

To Upgrading Your Life To The Next Level,
Signature

P.S. As silly as it may sound - **You Only Live Once -** and it should be spent the way you want to, right?

===> LINK

Discover the key to better health, an increase in business, incredible relationships and unbreakable confidence in yourself.

Avoid going down the wrong path, wasting years, feeling unhappy and stressed out. I'll show you the way!

==>LINK

Email 5: [Day 4 Email 2]

SL 1 - Did you miss this?
SL 2 - Oops… this missed you?

I figured you may have missed this…

So, to make sure you don't get left out, I wanted to send it to you again.

But remember, this is your **LAST DAY** to take action on it.

If won't be here tomorrow for you to change your mind.

Here's what I'm talking about, the last email I sent you:

-----------------Copy & Paste From Previous Email---------------

I've been poor.

However recently, I've become wealthier.

And I can honestly say, I would rather be upset with money than enthusiastically poor.

You see, no matter how much money I make, there's still people depending on me.

I could either - have enough money to take care of everyone <u>**or I could make enough just to pay my own bills and absolutely nothing else.**</u>

I couldn't take it anymore, looking at family members who were in debt and couldn't afford their house let alone groceries for next week.

It's devastating to watch people who are close to you, run their lives into the ground and be left with nothing.

But it's even worse, when you're in the same boat and you can't help them out.

You're both just sinking, with a tiny bucket to scoop the water out of your boat.

What if you could make a simple change to your daily routine and generate an increasingly amount of business, plus turn your relationships around *for good?*

Well, after seeing this - **you'll be SHOCKED with how easy it is.**

==>LINK

In fact, it's the same exact path I've taken to turn my life around, build myself into a self-made millionaire, and find the [woman/man] of my dreams.

And I can assume, since you're reading this - you want to see some of the same results I've seen.

So, take advantage while you can...

==>LINK

Today is literally your LAST chance to see this.

After this, your email will be forgotten and this link won't work anymore.

If you want to make the change in your life you need to become a self-made millionaire…

… then you'll want to click over now.

To Upgrading Your Life To The Next Level,
Signature

P.S. As silly as it may sound - **You Only Live Once** - and it should be spent the way you want to, right?

===> LINK

Discover the key to better health, an increase in business, incredible relationships and unbreakable confidence in yourself.

Avoid going down the wrong path, wasting years, feeling unhappy and stressed out. I'll show you the way!

==>LINK

~ Email Sequence 4 ~

Email 1:
SL 1 - Why didn't you start this sooner?
SL 2 - Why the wealthy get richer...

Have you been wondering what makes "wealthy" people so different from the rest?

===> LINK TEXT SAME AS SUBJECT LINE

Contrary to popular belief, becoming wealthy isn't just about *taking action*.

You see, your mindset and attitude towards yourself, will have a huge impact on your actions, as well.

[INSERT YOUR NAME] here...

I remember the days where I would work my butt off, checking tasks off my list and doing every single thing *by myself.*

It's a little hard to accomplish my bigger goals when I have so many little tasks piling up on a daily basis.

If you're anything like me, you're exhausted at the end of the day and in dire need of a "breather."

And when you realize you didn't accomplish much or had enough time to get to your more important goals, you get frustrated.

The thing is, when you become overwhelmed with your work, it shows in your performance.

You'll start to be more sluggish with your projects, you'll notice most tasks were only 75% completed and you no longer have the passion you used to, in the beginning.

===> LINK TEXT SAME AS SUBJECT LINE

Once your attitude takes a plunge and your mindset is stuck on "negative"...

... you'll have a harder time building a successful business or developing *healthy* relationships.

Everything in your life is connected and you'll start to see a domino effect, where your life becomes less enjoyable, you can't look at yourself in the mirror and you feel like you're no longer fulfilling your dreams.

There's a better way to live, than living in misery.

And controlling your emotions is the key to a better lifestyle.

So, if you're ready to make a change and improve the quality of your life - starting with the right mindset - you may want to check this out!

===> LINK TEXT SAME AS SUBJECT LINE

I took a leap, made a difference with my life and now I'm *extremely happy.*

If I can do it, you can too!

Here's how you can get started:

===> LINK TEXT SAME AS SUBJECT LINE

To Living An Unbeatable Life,
Signature

P.S. I promise, once you click over...you'll be AMAZED by how easy it is to make this simple change in your life.

But you'll be even more **SHOCKED** with the results you start seeing from it.

You'll be asking yourself, why you didn't start this sooner!

===> LINK TEXT SAME AS SUBJECT LINE

Email 2:

SL 1 - Key to improving your life...
SL 2 - Voices in my head?

Keep your head up, life can always get better for you.

===> LINK TEXT SAME AS SUBJECT LINE

You're literally one step away from making a *phenomenal* change in your life.

I'm not talking about making a change you don't like.

No, I'm talking about *improving* your life and taking it to the next level.

Something you've only dreamed about...until now.

You see, there's always a way to upgrade from where you're at right now.

It's not hard and if you stick with me, I'll show you the way.

In fact, I've followed this simple strategy for years now and the results still blow me away.

I love waking up to the life I live now.

I'm happy, excited about reaching my goals, accomplishing my dreams and absolutely LOVE the relationships I've built over the years.

Not just a life partner, but connecting with better business partners, connecting with family on a new level and finally feeling like you *belong*.

I know how hard it can be to quiet the voices in your head telling you, *"you can't do this."*

Those voices were yelling at me almost every second of every day.

It's frustrating and downright depressing.

But once you can drown those voices out.

You can reach past your personal limitations and break out of the chains you feel have been holding you back.

It's time to turn your life around and finally see what happiness can bring you.

How can you do this?

Simple, click this link for the step-by-step strategy I've personally used.

To Living An Unbeatable Life,
Signature

P.S. It may sound like a giant leap, but I can promise you - you'll be AMAZED with the results.

===> LINK TEXT SAME AS SUBJECT LINE

If you're ready for a change, then this was made for you.

Or you could continue down the path you're on and manage the evil thoughts in your head, by yourself.

Hopefully they'll let you succeed, but we both know it's unlikely to happen.

===> LINK TEXT SAME AS SUBJECT LINE

Email 3:
SL 1 - How to succeed without overworking?
SL 2 - Work less and make more?

Overworking yourself is actually sabotaging your chances of turning your dreams into a reality.

===> LINK TEXT SAME AS SUBJECT LINE

If you're too busy trying to accomplish the smaller things in life, **you forget about the more important tasks on your list.**

You could be seeing an increase in your social life but a decrease in your business.

Or *vise versa*.

But keeping the balance is what can be a little more difficult.

You see, it's not about working as many hours as your body will allow.

It's more about what you can accomplish in a shorter amount of time.

Why?

Simple. Don't you want more time to enjoy life?

You could go on a permanent vacation and make money on your own time...

...maybe even spend more time with family and friends...

...or put the extra time towards building a new business.

In fact, there's people making millions but only working 2 hours a day.

However, there's people working **18 hours day and not even making 50k a year.**

It's a tragedy and I don't want you to become one of those people.

I want to take you to the next and show you exactly what it takes to get there.

So, I want to introduce to something **AMAZING**, which has helped me turn my life around and finally feel happy about where I'm at in life.

And I'm finally looking forward to my future and the plans I have laid out for myself.

==> Here's What I'm Talking About...

If you see even 1/10 the results I did, you're life will get an extreme makeover and you'll experience some massive enhancements where you need them.

Get started now and start living the lifestyle you've dreamed about.

==> Here's What I'm Talking About...

To Living An Unbeatable Life,
Signature

P.S. You have two choices:

You could take what I just said, make the first step and discover what it takes to tap into a powerful strategy for turning your dream life into a reality...

===> LINK TEXT SAME AS SUBJECT LINE

...or you could ignore it ALL, keep living your life and 2 weeks down the road, you'll be sitting at your computer wondering why you didn't start sooner.

You can either take action now or kick yourself in the butt for not doing sooner!

==> Here's What I'm Talking About

Email 4:

SL 1 - How to become a self-made ...
SL 2 - (Revealed) Reverse-Engineering Success?

What if you could reverse engineer what it takes to become a Millionaire?

===> LINK TEXT SAME AS SUBJECT LINE

Frankly, it's easier than you think...

You see, there's a list of things that make a millionaire different from the rest of the world.

And it's not just the amount of money they make.

In fact, they have a completely different mindset.

They've tapped into their true potential, they don't let anything come between them and success.

I've never seen anything like it.

My friend Eric has a hustle nobody can beat.

He's been through the roughest times and came out on top because he didn't let any of get him down.

You see, to become a HUGE success, <u>**you'll need perseverance, determination and a little motivation.**</u>

If you can't keep yourself on track, you'll start to veer off the path and slowly fail along the way.

I don't want this to happen to you.

So, here's a simple strategy you can follow:

===> LINK TEXT SAME AS SUBJECT LINE

I literally follow it everyday, and it's opened up doors for me I never thought possible.

I'm super enthusiastic now, I can finally say I make a butt load of money, I'm truly happy with my relationships…

… my health has never been better and my life is ultimately unbeatable at this point.

===> LINK TEXT SAME AS SUBJECT LINE

To Living An Unbeatable Life,
Signature

P.S. Look, you can either waste your time running yourself thin, exhausting your health, generating the bare minimum in income...

...or you could turn this all around and follow the steps you'll see on the next screen.

I promise you, it's not hard. I did it myself and it's been proven to work by countless others, as well!

===> LINK TEXT SAME AS SUBJECT LINE

Email 5:

SL 1 - The lazy way to fortunes?
SL 2 - How To Unleash Your Power...

You may not know this already, but I can't keep it a secret any longer.

===> LINK TEXT SAME AS SUBJECT LINE

I know how it feels to be at "rock bottom," in debt and pretty depressed with life.

It's not charming and it drove everyone away from me.

Why?

Simple, people don't like to be surrounded by misery and **nobody enjoys the company of someone who is depressed.**

I couldn't keep a relationship and I was having a hard time keeping money in my bank account.

Everything was demanding more money from me, while I still couldn't find another way to increase my supply of it.

I was running out of options and extremely desperate for a solution.

This is when I met Eric.

He helped open my eyes to the endless possibilities, showing me which path to take to achieve my goals and how to become a self-made millionaire.

I thought it wasn't possible, an ordinary/boring [guy/gal] like myself, becoming a success where people know who I am and look up to me for advice in life.

I now know what it feels like to enjoy life, be happy for a change and help others become happy as well.

Now it's your turn to tap into your true potential and discover true happiness for a change.

Ready for it?

===> LINK TEXT SAME AS SUBJECT LINE

I promise, I'll be with you every step of the way.

But you have to be serious about making a change or it won't work.

==You can't just put in half the effort and expect 100% of the results.==

You'll need to make a decision whether you want to become a better version of yourself or go on living the way you are right now.

===> LINK TEXT SAME AS SUBJECT LINE

I'm confident you'll make the right decision.

To Living An Unbeatable Life,
Signature

P.S. Listen, we both know there are a ton of people living their dream lives.

Luckily, you don't have to be the person looking in from the outside, *anymore*.

You can join the club and become a *happy camper* yourself.

Ready to make a change?

Then click the link, this is your LAST chance!

===> LINK TEXT SAME AS SUBJECT LINE

~ Email Sequence 5 ~
- Abandoned Cart Emails -

Email 1: You may have forgotten about this...

Is this a better time?

Recently, you showed interest in Luna Serum.

But something came up and you weren't able to complete your order.

===> **Click Here To Finish Your Order**

[NAME] here,

I wanted to stop by and see if this was a better time.

You see, I completely understand, **life has a way of throwing a ton of things at you all at once.**

Stuff pops up and interrupts your train of thought, putting your wants and needs - on hold.

Well, **here's your chance** to get what you've been waiting for and finish your order for your Luna Serum, right now.

But, you may want to be quick about it, life may throw you another curve ball at any moment and I wouldn't want you to miss out on this.

Are you ready to rejuvenate your skin, feel younger - **and look like it too**?

===> **Click Here To Finish Your Order**

To healthier looking skin,
Signature

P.S. Here's that link again:

===> **Click Here To Finish Your Order**

Email 2: Is the summer heat damaging your skin?

Are you suffering from dry skin?

It's more common than you think.

[NAME] here,

You see, **your skin is your body's first line of defense.**

So, it's super important to keep it healthy and strong.

Wouldn't you agree?

In fact, I know you've been looking for the perfect **solution to improving your skin and looking healthier than ever.**

How?

Simple, you showed interest in Luna Serum.

But for some reason, you couldn't complete your order.

===> **Click Here To Finish Your Order**

Look, I know things come up sometimes and distract you from what you're doing.

It happens to all of us.

This is why, I'm stopping by to make sure you get the chance to complete your order - **at a better time for you.**

===> **Click Here To Finish Your Order**

But you may want to hurry, there's a limited supply left and I don't want you to miss out!

It's going to change your outlook on skin care and make it easier for you to maintain healthy skin.

To healthier (younger looking) skin,
Signature

P.S. Here's the link again, quick before they're sold out:

===> **Click Here To Finish Your Order**

Email 3: Are you mad at me?

Did I do something wrong?

It's ok, tell me the truth.

You see, I tend to repel people sometimes.

And I wanted to make sure you weren't one of those people.

In fact, I want to personally help you as much as I can.

Recently, you showed an interest in Luna Serum and I wanted to give you another chance to get it.

Listen, I know things happen.

Life is busy, and can be seriously hectic sometimes.

If you're anything like me, something probably distracted you and then you forgot how to get back to the page you were on.

Well, it's your lucky day.

===> **Click Here To Finish Your Order**

And before you start to freak out, thinking I'm crazy for showing you this again…

…you should complete your order - they're selling out fast and I would hate to see you miss out on this.

Your skin shouldn't suffer for my mistakes.

If I've upset you, please take this as my apology and "gift" to you.

===> **Click Here To Finish Your Order**

Your skin will thank you for it!

Imagine what it will feel like to see a younger looking you in the mirror.

You'll be picture ready and happier than you've ever been.

Complete your order right now!

===> **Click Here To Finish Your Order**

To healthier (younger looking) skin,
Signature

P.S. Don't forget, this is your very LAST chance to get this.

And they're selling out pretty fast, quick get yours now before they're all sold out!

===> **Click Here To Finish Your Order**

- Value/Soft Pitch Emails -

Email 1: proven to enhance the natural glow of your skin...

What is the first thing someone sees when they look at you?

Simple - **your skin.**

So, you want it looking *good,* right?

The bad new is, your skin can show the world how unhealthy you are.

The good news is, there's ways to reverse this.

But more on that later.

Have you noticed your face and neck breaking out when you're super stressed out?

Or how about the small red spots that show up when you're anxious, excited and even when you're upset?

There's nothing to be ashamed about.

This happens to everyone.

One way to help reduce the effects of stress on your skin is - **by reducing the amount of stress you're taking on.**

I know this may sound obvious, but sometimes people don't realize how much stress they have in their lives.

And how easy it can be to remove it.

When you start to feel like you're stressing out, try to take a step back and explain to yourself why you're really upset or overwhelmed.

Then ask yourself if you could use some help.

If you can get the work done in half the time and cut the workload in half, then I would suggest asking for help.

This can easily reduce the anxiety you feel when you're drowning in tasks to do and can't seem to get it all done, by yourself.

For those super stressful days, try using a calming cream or **[INSERT PRODUCT]**, proven to enhance the natural glow of your skin and keep it feeling healthy throughout the day.

===>Get started now to see results even faster!

To feeling (& looking) healthier than ever,
Signature

P.S. If you have a moment, I would love to hear about your success stories. Send me a message back about a time, you were able to conquer stress and enjoy the rest of your day.

I look forward to hearing all about it!

Email 2: Becoming more and more tired as the days drag on? Reverse the effects...

Are you not getting enough sleep lately?

When you become tired, your body starts to show it.

And the first place it pops up is - your skin.

You start to get baggy eyes, wrinkles, and your color will start to fade, making your look sick.

If you don't want to look like a zombie walking around the office...you may want to get a little more sleep.

I know, it sounds *super simple.*

But, most women have a hard time falling asleep and staying asleep for the right amount of time.

Frankly, it's damaging their health.

You see, your body needs time to heal and rejuvenate itself, overnight.

If it doesn't get the appropriate time to heal - it goes into overdrive trying to make up for lost energy without replenishing it.

We can easily say, this is terrible for your body and mind.

One thing women have been trying lately is "Melatonin" to help them fall asleep.

In fact, our bodies already have a supply of it - it's the chemical that tells our bodies when to go to sleep and when to wake up.

But if you're having trouble sleeping, then you're supply is running low.

Give it a try!

Another way to help improve your energy and feel refreshed each morning is by using **[INSERT PRODUCT].**

It can help reduce wrinkles, stress lines and reverse the effects "lack of sleep" will have on your skin.

===>**Get started now to see results even faster!**

To feeling (& looking) healthier,
Signature

P.S. Don't forget to send me a message, telling me how it went with the Melatonin and **[INSERT PRODUCT].** I look forward to hearing all about it!

Email 3: What fruit will help you look healthier than ever...

Did you know, your health has a connection to your skin?

You see, when your organs are unhealthy, your skin shows it.

You can start to look sickly, pale and feel drained of energy.

But the worst part is, when the wrinkles start to show up.

When your health begins to decline, your body is unbalanced and will strip you of certain nutrients to ensure survival.

Nutrients like Vitamin C, Vitamin D, and many more.

Before you freak out - something as simple as a detox may be the key to increasing your health.

And once your body is healthy on the inside, it will show on the outside.

The best foods to eat when you're looking to detox are:

1. Lemons
2. Oranges
3. Grapefruit
4. & Pineapple

You may have noticed these are all tropical/citrus fruit.

The reason for this is because these are all filled with Vitamin C and will help increase the benefits of your detox while replenishing the nutrients your body needs to thrive.

Another one is watermelon, not only is it filled with Vitamin C - it's also comprised of mostly water.

But that's another story for another time.

And remember to fill me in on all the details about how successful your detox went.

To feeling (& looking) healthier,
Signature

P.S. Another way to replenish the nutrients in your skin is by applying **[INSERT PRODUCT]** once, daily.

For visibly healthier looking skin, stay consistent with your routine and *have fun* with your detox.

[INSERT COUPON LINK]

Email #4: How you apply your makeup, could be damaging your skin...

It's true!

If you're blotching your makeup on…

…it could be damaging your skin and causing your pores to clog up.

All in all - it's not a pretty sight.

The best way to apply your makeup is to massage it on.

Yes - massage!

Slowly rub it on, in circular motions, and gently apply the makeup thoroughly across your face.

This applies to your moisturizer, toner, concealer and any other product you use on your face.

The best part is, this little trick will kick your circulation into gear and will help your skin feel healthier than ever.

You see, your skin is very delicate - it can only take so much torture until it starts to *crack*.

And when we say crack - we mean wrinkles, dark spots, baggy skin, and more.

If you're looking for a better way to give your skin that refreshing feeling, then try out **[INSERT PRODUCT]**.

It's been helping women across the world - reverse the effects of aging and it even, helped remove some of their blotchy sun spots.

===>**Get started now to see results even faster!**

But remember, when you're applying it to your face - use a massaging, gentle pressure to avoid damaging your skin any further.

To feeling (& looking) healthier,
Signature

P.S. I would love to know what you think about **[INSERT PRODUCT]** and how it's helped you. Send me a reply message with the details. I look forward to hearing from you.

- Pitch Email -

Email 1: Are you suffering with severe, dry skin?

Do you keep up with the weather?

I mean seriously keep up with it.

You see, our summers have been getting some record-breaking heat waves and the winters are no better.

Why am I talking about the weather?

Simple, too many women these days don't connect weather to dry, damaged skin.

And frankly, weather has a HUGE effect on our skin.

Daily *moisturizer* is **your best defense for dry skin.**

The most commonly misused "protection" is - sun block.

In fact, most people don't use it at all.

And others use it too much.

Look, we both know, your body needs a certain amount of sun each day to build a healthy level of Vitamin D.

But if you overdo it, you can get some serious burns, causing your skin to fry and put you in severe pain.

If you're anything like me, you've experienced a couple sunburns in your life.

And they weren't pleasant to have.

The worst part is, the itchiness and you can't scratch it or you'll be in more pain.

You see, the itchiness is actually your skin healing itself and if you start to scratch, you'll interrupt the healing process - making your body start all over again.

You can avoid this painful situation by wearing a little bit of sunblock when you go outside, especially if you're going to be outside for a long period of time.

One way to get sunblock into your daily routine is by using a moisturizer with a bit of sunblock in it, like **[INSERT PRODUCT].**

This way, you're putting it on without thinking about it and you don't have to stress throughout the day whether your face is going to burn or not.

===>Get started now to see results even faster!

Again - *daily moisturizer* is **your best defense for dry skin.**

Give it a try and enjoy the sunny days for a change!

To feeling (& looking) healthier,
Signature

P.S. If you're going to be in the sun for hours, I would recommend applying it more than once to ensure maximum protection.

===>**Get started now to see results even faster!**

Don't forget to let me know how everything goes and fill me in on the details of your next "sunny" adventure! You can send me a reply message directly from here.

- Value/Soft Pitch Emails -

Email 1: **What is the most "well-kept" secret for skin care...**

If you're anything like me, you have to wash your face daily and sometimes two, three times a day.

Why? Simple, oily skin can turn into *dirty* skin, real quick.

If I don't keep up with washing my face and managing the oil, then I look like I haven't taken a shower in weeks.

No joke.

The worst part is, when my skin is super oily or I sweat too much, I'm prone to get acne.

And it's not pretty.

It's a large one, sitting square in the middle of my face, screaming at everyone to look at it.

It makes me feel like a teenager again!

Want to know a well-kept secret for healthier skin, and how to avoid "adult" acne?

First, make sure nobody is within reading or hearing distance.

Now, keep an open mind and don't laugh.

The best "exercise" or remedy for your skin is, sex.

You see, when you're having sex - your endorphins are in high drive, which helps you release bad toxins and give your skin the natural glow every woman is envious of.

The best part is, it helps boost the natural protection your skin gives you and easily helps you avoid "adult" acne.

Don't just take my word for it - test it out for yourself.

In the meantime, here's another uncommonly known remedy to get healthier looking (& feeling) skin - **[INSERT PRODUCT].**

It's been proven to give you the same natural glow you can get from a simple "exercise" without actually doing all the work.

===>**Get started now to see results even faster!**

Just simply massage it on your face (daily) for maximum benefits and skin protection.

To healthier looking (& feeling) skin,
Signature

P.S. [INSERT PRODUCT] is a well kept secret within a tight knit group, and I want to give you exclusive access to it. Take advantage while you can - they're going pretty fast.

Email 2: Acne strikes again! Reverse the effects with...

Have you had a zit, recently?

The most commonly asked question is,

"Should I pop it or should I leave it alone?"

Well, contrary to popular belief - and you didn't hear it from us - popping a zit can actually be GOOD sometimes.

Now, there are certain situations where it's bad, as well.

So, you need to be very careful with how you treat a zit.

It can either become smooth, healthy skin or a nasty looking scar.

Have you noticed, your acne tends to show up when you're super stressed out or anxious about something?

This is more common than you think.

And acne does NOT discriminate between age.

You could be 2 with acne and you could be 72 with acne.

It happens. And it's nothing to be ashamed about.

Here's what you'll want to do:

Step #1: Give the spot a gentle squeeze - ONLY if it's white on top - using two cotton swabs, gently press on both sides until it pops

Step #2: Once you've cleaned off the gunk, dab a little bit of salicylic acid treatment on top

Make sure you're washing your face daily, and keeping up with a moisturizer to help your skin become healthier without damaging your skin in the process.

A great one we would recommend is **[INSERT PRODUCT]**, which has been hearing some pretty great reviews.

===>**Get started now to see results even faster!**

Here's what one woman said about it:

[INSERT TESTIMONIAL]

Remember, your skin is your body's first line of defense...so keep it healthy and strong for the best protection possible.

To healthier looking (& feeling) skin,
Signature

P.S. I look forward to hearing about your latest adventures and how **[INSERT PRODUCT]** has helped your skin along the way. Send me a message with all the details. Talk soon!

Email 3: Drink this for refreshed, glowing skin all day long...

Rise and shine.

Grab a cup of tea and take a moment to enjoy your morning.

It's a brand new day, your hair is looking fabulous as usual...

...but your skin may not be up to par.

If you've been stressed out lately or you've been sweating a ton, your skin could be suffering from it.

Besides washing your face every day, you can do something as simple as drinking a cup of tea to enhance the natural beauty of your skin.

In fact, tea helps our bodies from the inside - out.

Some teas can even help lower risk of heart disease and reduce cholesterol, while some other teas have anti-bacterial qualities and some help fight sleep issues.

The best part is, there's so many options to choose from and each one has it's own powerful benefits.

But there's something you may not know about tea.

You see, drinking tea is also great for your skin.

Before you get overwhelmed with all the choices, here's 5 teas you can drink to help improve the health of your skin and keep it looking beautiful:

1 - Chamomile Tea - Great for sleep which is essential for natural glowing skin

2 - Jasmine Tea - Packed with immune boosting properties, which can help reduce the effects of aging

3 - Green Tea - Surprisingly, it's filled with sun-fighting elements and will help protect your skin from harsh UV rays

4 - Dandelion Tea - full of antioxidants & immunity enhancing properties which helps your skin stay young and fresh

5 - Peppermint Tea - It's not just good for an upset stomach, it also has powerful benefits for combatting oily skin

The weird thing is, you can drink them, apply them directly to your skin or even use extracts to see significant results.

For even better results, before drinking a cup of tea, massage a dab of **[INSERT PRODUCT]** on your face.

It can enhance your natural glow, reduce dark spots, and might even help fight sun or smoking damage.

===>Get started now to see results even faster!

This makes it worth trying!

To healthier feeling (& looking) skin,
Signature

P.S. Which tea was your favorite? I would love to hear about the results you've seen from drinking more tea. Send me a quick message with some of the benefits you've experienced from this.

Thank you for your time!

Email 4: Why chocolate is actually good for you…

Surprisingly, everyone tries to keep this a secret.

I would rather the whole world knew, especially the women.

Why?

Well, it's the one thing almost every woman craves and is told to avoid.

You know what I'm talking about - CHOCOLATE.

But, you have to get the right kind.

The rumor has been, chocolate causes acne.

Good news - this rumor has never been proven to be more than just a rumor.

In fact, DARK chocolate is very healthy for you.

You see, dark chocolate is filled with antioxidants which help your skin. Plus, eating a small piece will send a whole army of "satisfied and happy" feelings to your brain.

And remember, being happy has an amazing effect on your skin, as well!

So eat up!

There's even dark chocolate covered almonds, some have honey in them and a few have coconut flakes.

To improve your results even more try out **[INSERT PRODUCT]**, it only takes a small amount each morning and you'll see some amazing results!

===>**<u>Get started now to see results even faster!</u>**

Enjoy and talk soon.

To healthier feeling (& looking) skin,
Signature

P.S. Which type of dark chocolate is your favorite? I've been wondering which ones to recommend but I don't want to only say, my bias opinion.

I look forward to hearing what you think.

Don't forget to give **<u>[INSERT PRODUCT]</u>** a try.

- Pitch Email -

Email 1: **Looking for the key to healthier skin?**

It's frustrating to clean your face on a daily basis and still feel like your skin isn't healthy.

I know what it likes to spend countless hours looking in the mirror, trying every face wash and skin care product I could find.

And still not see the results I was looking for.

It's down right depressing, especially when the acne starts to pop up more often.

I thought I was over those years.

I don't want to feel or look like a teenager, with dark spots, dry skin, acne or super oily skin.

The worst part is having friends who don't understand what you're going through.

You see, my best friend had the perfect skin - flawless and beautiful.

One day I got up the courage to ask her how she does it and here's what she said.

"It's simple. I dab a little bit of **[INSERT PRODUCT]** on my face each morning and massage it in...then go about my day. It works wonders for me without stressing about it."

I couldn't resist trying it out for myself.

And I have to tell you - it worked like crazy, even for me.

If it can work for, it can work for you too!

===>**<u>Get started now to see results even faster!</u>**

This face cream isn't like the rest, it's not going to clog your pores or cause more acne - it actually helps relieve your skin of dark spots, reduce acne, improve wrinkles and even help protect against the sun's harsh rays.

It's been proven by numerous scientists to work, take advantage of it while you can!

I look forward to hearing about how everything works out for you.

To healthier feeling (& looking) skin,
Signature

P.S. Are you as excited as I am, for you to have healthier, glamorous skin? I can't wait to see what you think about it.

===>**Get started now to see results even faster!**

- Value/Soft Pitch Emails -

Email 1: Reverse the effects summer weather has on your skin...

Having trouble with these serious heat waves we've been getting?

It's that time again - summer time!

And it's seriously HOT.

Even with 98% humidity, your skin would dry out, causing some severe wrinkles and making your skin look like a desert.

It's not pretty and frankly, it can be pretty painful if it gets out of hand.

How can you avoid the "shriveled" look?

Simple - **drink more water.**

It may seem like this is common sense, but you would be surprised by how many women forget to drink water throughout the day.

You see, one glass a day just doesn't cut it.

In fact, your body will start to practically, starve if you only drink one glass of water a day.

You really need about 10-16 glasses of water per day to boost your health and enhance your skin's natural glow.

The worst part is, if you don't drink enough water you may even experience some headaches due to a lack of electrolytes and dehydration.

It happens more often than you think.

And you may not even notice the headache is coming from a lack of water.

Another super easy way to evade the effects of dry weather and the harsh summer seasons is with **[INSERT PRODUCT].**

With just a small dab of it, you can massage it onto your face for extra protection against the relentless sun and added moisture during those extra hot days!

===>Click Here For Our BEST Protective Moisturizer

Now you can enjoy your time in the sun without worrying about the effects it will have on your skin.

To healthier feeling (& looking) skin,
Signature

P.S. In your opinion, what does a "perfect" beach day look like?

I look forward to hearing what you think. Quick, send me a message before you forget and something distracts you.

Email 2: Does the effects of aging show when you look in the mirror?

When is the last time you looked in the mirror?

This morning, last night, 15 minutes ago?

If you're anything like me, every time you look in the mirror you question what you can do to make your appearance look a little better.

Aging hasn't done me any favors, the wrinkles were adding up and the dark spots were starting to make me look very blotchy.

Frankly, makeup wasn't helping and I was running out of options.

You see, I've already tried everything out there.

From a body lotion to an expensive face cream - NOTHING worked.

I still didn't the results I was looking for.

And I was wasting a ton of money in the process.

It's frustrating and downright depressing.

If this sounds familiar, don't freak out.

It took me awhile but I've found the perfect solution.

It's called "relaxation" and it's practically, unheard of.

I'm not kidding.

In fact, here's your mission - if you choose to accept it - take a full weekend and treat yourself to some "you" time.

Start it off first thing Friday night.

You can rub a face mask on like **[INSERT PRODUCT],** and take a long, hot bubble bath.

Trust me, you'll thank me later for this.

You'll be amazed with how calming, and beneficial it is to have a relaxing, spa day for yourself.

It's even better when you don't have to smell the harsh chemicals in a salon or listen to all the loud customers coming in and out of those places.

This way, you have a quiet and calm atmosphere to help put you in a positive mood.

Remember, the happier you are, the happier your skin is too!

Spend the whole weekend giving yourself different spa treatments, starting with the mask and ending with a pedicure.

Once your weekend is over, you'll be shocked with how amazing you feel on Monday.

And you'll be surprised by how many compliments you get for how GREAT your skin is looking.

===>Get Better Looking Skin In Less Time

To healthier feeling (& looking) skin,
Signature

P.S. What else would you include in your next "spa day?" I prefer to start with my toes, let them dry and then put on my face mask. What do you do?

Quick, send me a message before you forget and something distracts you.

~ Email Sequence 6 ~

- Email 1 -
Subject Line #1: here's your free book....
Subject Line #2: you asked for a free book, here it is....

Did you get your free eBook?

Well, here it is:

[INSERT LINK HERE]

I hope you get the chance to read through it today.

It's not too long but it's filled to the rim with useful information and powerful techniques to help you trim the extra pounds you've been carrying around.

I've made it my mission to help you see the results you want without putting you through bootcamp to get them.

And this is where the book will come in handy. It delivers exactly what you need to know, in an easy to read bundle.

Follow along, take action where needed and enjoy the side effects of weight loss like, more energy and a positive mindset.

To Your Weight Loss Goals,
Signature

P.S. Look, we both know the worldwide web is LOADED with different methods for losing weight, toning your body and getting in better shape...but it would take you hours to sort through it all and pinpoint what will work for you.

I want to help you cut this workload in half, and give you a solution I know will work for you.

You'll discover the full details within this book: [INSERT LINK HERE]

Dig in and enjoy!

- Email 2 -
Subject Line #1: Did you get the book, revealing weight loss secrets yet?
Subject Line #2: Have you read this book yet?

I can only imagine, you have a million things going on right now...

...so, I'm going to keep this short and sweet.

Has anyone told you how incredible you are lately?

You're going out of your way to make a difference and change the way you feel about yourself.

You're challenging yourself to think outside of the box and find a better way to lose weight without overdoing it physically or mentally.

You see, there's a higher number of women who take the wrong route when it comes to losing weight.

They put in all this effort, going on a diet, doing exercises everyday and still not seeing the results they want.

All of their efforts were wasted.

Sound familiar?

Then you'll definitely want to read this: [INSERT LINK HERE]
It's completely FREE and all yours!

Take your time, read each chapter carefully and take action where needed.

What you're about to discover will change the way you look at "dieting" and make your journey to slim & fit...much easier!

Give it your complete attention: [INSERT LINK HERE]

To Your Weight Loss Goals,
Signature

P.S. Remember when I said, it's my mission to help you see the results you *want?* Well, I wasn't lying. OVer the next few days, I'm going to be sending you some helpful weight loss hacks, dieting tips, and even some tools you can use to lose weight, **effortlessly.**

Keep an eye out, you don't want to miss them!

- Email 3 -
Subject Line #1: Have you tried this healthier "comfort" food?
Subject Line #2: A healthier way to make your "comfort" foods...

I hope by now, you've had a chance to read your new book.

This one: [INSERT LINK]

Anyways, I wanted to stop by and give you some additional help.

You see, I know how hard it is to give up those "comfort" foods you depend on so much.

It's difficult and downright stressful.

However, you don't need to eliminate the complete meal or snack.

You can just substitute the bad ingredients for healthier ones.

In fact, one the best substitutes you can use is Almond Flour.

When you bake with it, it's delicious...

When you fry up some chicken tenders with it, it's mouth-watering...

And when you use it for pancakes, it's literally out of this world *good*.

You don't even notice the difference and you'll be eating healthier without even realizing it.

There's "Coconut Flour" as well.

Here's a couple difference between the two:

- Almond flour has more calories than coconut flour
- Almond flour has fewer carbs and fiber than coconut flour
- They're BOTH Gluten Free

- Both are a good source of Iron, Manganese, and Magnesium
- And they both have a Low Glycemic Score

Depending on what you're looking for...more fiber vs less calories, you can stay fit and stay on track by using these two substitutes.

Give it a try. You never know how much better it is, until you try it for yourself.

To Your Weight Loss Goals,
Signature

P.S. It's better when you have people pushing you to the finish line, and have friends there to keep you on track as well. Join our FREE group of weight loss enthusiasts, just like you, challenging themselves to lose a few extra pounds and become the healthiest version of themselves.

It doesn't hurt, to ask questions and share your story to help motivate others to take the first step to a healthier life.

- Email 4 -
Subject Line #1: Losing weight is as simple as drinking...
Subject Line #2: You can easily lose weight by simply drinking...

Did you know you can lose weight by drinking more water?

No, seriously.

Water is pretty amazing.

It's less calories than soft drinks, it has less sugar and it's better for you.

Dear friend,

Frankly, more water in the long run, means less body fat.

And when you start seeing the pounds melt away, you'll start feeling better about yourself.

More confident. More appreciative. And Even Happier with the way you look in just about *any* outfit.

Look, we both know you already need water to survive. If you drink just a little more, you can see some pretty incredible results.

I know it's hard to wing yourself off of those other drinks, so here's 6 ways you can make drinking water, a habit:

1. Drink a glass of water with each meal
2. Carry a water bottle with you throughout the day
3. Keep water on your desk at work
4. When you feel like a snack, try drinking water first
5. Instead of a tea or soft drink, have a glass of water
6. Track your water intake. Record how many glasses you're drinking a day

Water is going to be one of your best tools for weight loss. Why?

Simple, it helps repress cravings, suppresses your appetite and helps you stay away from sugary drinks.

I know it's hard to imagine, water being such a big help with your weight loss goals.

But it's true!

So, try drinking a few more glasses of water everyday and you'll be amazed with the results.

To Your Weight Loss Goals,
Signature

P.S. Tell me all about your success and how these tips have helped you personally. You can connect directly with me here: [INSERT LINK HERE]

- Email 5 -
Subject Line #1: Are you weight loss efforts being wasted?
Subject Line #2: STOP Looking For Weight Loss Secrets, this will...

Looking for easier ways to lose weight?

Dear friend,

What if you could lose weight without joining a gym by just adding a super food to your diet…

…would you do it?

I know I would.

It's seems like a no-brainer. Add a piece of food to my eating habits or work my butt off trying to lose a few extra pounds…

….hmmm, which one would you choose?

Well, before you make any serious decisions, here's 7 super foods you can add to your diet to start seeing better results:

1. **Blueberries -** Filled with Antioxidants, Vitamin C, Fiber & Help You Slim Down (Add them salads, smoothies, and breakfast)
2. **Bananas** - Filled with Potassium & Vitamin B6 (From fighting depression, nausea and even stabilizing blood sugar levels between meals, bananas are one powerful fruit!)
3. **Apples** - Packed with Fiber (which can help you feel full and helps suppress your appetite)
4. **Spinach -** Packed with Magnesium, Iron & More (Helps eliminate cravings for unhealthy food)
5. **Salmon** - Filled with Omega 3's (Super low in calories, but super HIGH in protein)
6. **Grapefruit -** Packed with Vitamin C, Fiber & Folic Acid (Helps boost your metabolism and increase your immune system)
7. **Broccoli -** Filled with Vitamin C, Folic Acid and Iron (helps burn calories and build overall health)

Just by adding one or two of these to your daily meals, you can cut your calories and increase your chances of losing weight, tremendously.

If you don't get started now, you'll regret it in 2-3 weeks when you beat yourself up for procrastinating.

Losing weight, being healthy and feeling better about yourself is important.

To Your Weight Loss Goals,
Signature

P.S. Just a quick reminder, you'll be getting a couple more emails coming your way. These next ones will give you an insight into an even easier way to lose weight. Pay close attention to your inbox, you don't want to miss this. I promise it's worth it!

- Email 6 -
Subject Line #1: Simpler ways to trim fat without stepping foot in...
Subject Line #2: Sculpt your body to be the perfect "beach"body, the easy way...

Don't you wish it was easier to lose weight?

I mean come on.

Working out, sweating it off...just isn't cutting it.

Especially if you're overdoing it without realizing it.

You see, your body can only take so much stress before it starts to close down.

What do I mean by this?

Simple, if you're body isn't getting the right nutrients and you're exercising a lot, your immune system will start to feel overwhelmed.

You can get sick easier, you can gain weight easier, and you can start having severe mood swings...all from working out *too much.*

Before you freak out, there's plenty of ways to help you lose weight without stepping foot in a gym.

One sure way to help you lose weight and even balance your blood sugar levels is with Lean Health. [INSERT LINK HERE]

In fact, it's already helped thousands of women just like you, lose weight and slim down their body.

They're super happy with their new looks and amazing "beach" bodies.

I'm confident, you're going to love the results you get from this as well.

Imagine how many heads you'll be turning when you walk down the street looking like model.

You could have the body of your dreams, all without doing a single push up to get it.

Here's how you can get started: [INSERT LINK HERE]

To Your Weight Loss Goals,
Signature

P.S. If you're vitamin levels are low, your body won't have what it needs to break down the foods you eat and will instantly start converting it into fat to store for later.

Sound like something you want to avoid? Then this was made for you!

Here's how you can get started: [INSERT LINK HERE]

- Email 7 -
Subject Line #1: Have you seen success with your weight loss efforts?
Subject Line #2: Looking for an easier way to lose weight, then this is...

I've been bombarded with a ton of great success stories, from people during their weight loss process and thought about you.

You see, ultimately I care whether you're seeing results or not.

I would love to help you boost your chances of reaching well past your goals,

And to do this, I'm going to reveal more ways to boost your weight loss numbers.

You may have noticed with certain prescription medicines, you're experiencing some nasty weight gaining side effects.

The extra pounds you've been carrying could be caused by a number of medicines including the steroids used to treat Asthma, Inflammatory and even certain Antidepressants.

It's terrible when the medicine you've been prescribed is working against you.

So basically, you're medicine is sabotaging your efforts to melt away belly fat and damaging your chances of staying slim.

How can you change this around for *good*?

Simple.

You can increase your levels of Vitamin D, Magnesium and Phosphorous to help your stomach break down food into energy and avoid storing it as fat.

If you keep your levels balanced, your stomach will be able to perform at 100% and increase your metabolism to burn off the unwanted calories (without working out).

Without these nutrients, your stomach will become filled with acid and bad bacteria, increasing your fat intake and causing your body to store an even greater amount of it.

This means, more pudgy rolls, jiggly arms and not a slimmer, healthier body.

The cool part?

You can discover exactly what to add to your everyday eating habits…to counteract the nasty side effects of your prescription medicine and anything else that wants to sabotage your chances of staying slim.

Click the link below, get the full details and start building your dream body, right now.

Reverse the weight gain and start seeing better results
[INSERT LINK HERE]

To Your Weight Loss Goals,
Signature

P.S. If you're looking to increase your weight loss results and finally be happy to look at yourself naked in the mirror, without working out everyday….then this is perfect for you! Don't miss out.

Reverse the weight gain and start seeing better results
[INSERT LINK HERE]

CONCLUSION:

Alright, I've given you EVERYTHING.

Now, it's your turn.

You see, it would be mighty disappointing if you didn't take action with what you've learned from this book.

Why?

Simple, these techniques and methods have already been proven to work for myself or my clients.

However, since you've made it this far – I can safely say, I'm confident you're NOT the type to ignore what you've seen here.

You're probably the type to put it into action right away, excited to see what it can do for you.

But remember to always have fun, and never stop experimenting, you'll never know what new trick will work next.

Here's a quick recap of what we went over:

- ✓ The Copy Code has walked you through what you need to start generating leads,
- ✓ The Copy Code has shown you the importance of copywriting,
- ✓ The Copy Code has delivered valuable techniques you can use to write successful advertorials

I've shown you how to write a compelling advertorial and I've given you a look at what it takes to create a successful one.

You see, I've literally given you 8 advertorial samples in this book for you to use as inspiration.

Plus, I've included my email swipes for over 40 emails, you can use as insight and to help you write irresistible emails for your very own subscribers.

Did you find this helpful?

Leave a review or testimonial on my Facebook page at:

Facebook.com/TiffanyMoneyMind

Glossary: Marketing Terms to Improve Your Marketing Vocabulary

A
A/B Testing

This is the process of comparing two variations of a single variable to determine which performs best in order to help improve marketing efforts. This is often done in email marketing (with variations in the subject line or copy), calls-to-action (variations in colors or verbiage), and landing pages (variations in content).

Outside of marketing, you can use it to determine what tastes better on a peanut butter sandwich: jelly or fluff. (Learn how to run A/B tests here.)

Analytics

What I sometimes refer to as the "eyes" of inbound marketing, analytics is essentially the discovery and communication of meaningful patterns in data.

When referred to in the context of marketing, it's looking at the data of one's initiatives (website visitor reports, social, PPC, etc.), analyzing the trends, and developing actionable insights to make better informed marketing decisions. (Want to learn marketing analytics?

B
Bottom of the Funnel

Since we're going alphabetically, the last part of the funnel process is first! So, "bottoms up," I suppose.

The bottom of the funnel refers to a stage of the buying process leads reach when they're just about to close as new customers. They've identified a problem, have shopped around for possible solutions, and are very close to buying.

Typically, next steps for leads at this stage are a call from a sales rep, a demo, or a free consultation -- depending on what type of business is attempting to close the lead.

Bounce Rate

Website bounce rate: The percentage of people who land on a page on your website and then leave without clicking on anything else or navigating to any other pages on your site.

A high bounce rate generally leads to poor conversion rates because no one is staying on your site long enough to read your content or convert on a landing page (or for any other conversion event).

Email bounce rate: The rate at which an email was unable to be delivered to a recipient's inbox.

A high bounce rate generally means your lists are out-of-date or purchased, or they include many invalid email addresses.

In email, not all bounces are bad, so it's important to distinguish between hard and soft bounces before taking an email address off your list.

Buyer Persona

A semi-fictional representation of your ideal customer based on market research and real data about your existing customers.

While it helps marketers like you define their target audience, it can also help sales reps qualify leads.

C
Call-to-Action

A call-to-action is a text link, button, image, or some type of web link that encourages a website visitor to visit a landing page and become of lead. Some examples of CTAs are "Subscribe Now" or "Download the Whitepaper Today."

These are important for marketers because they're the "bait" that entices a website visitor to eventually become a lead. So, you can imagine that it's important to convey a very enticing, valuable offer on a call-to-action to better foster visitor-to-lead conversion.

Content

In relation to inbound marketing, content is a piece of information that exists for the purpose of being digested (not literally), engaged with, and shared.

Content typically comes in the form of a blog, video, social media post, photo, slideshow, or podcast, although there are plenty of over types out there.
From website traffic to lead conversion to customer marketing, content plays an indispensable role in a successful inbound marketing strategy.

Context

If content is king, then context is queen. Serving up valuable content is important, but ensuring that it's customized for the right audience is equally (if not more) important.

As buyers become more in control of what information they digest (again, not literally), it's important to deliver content that's contextually relevant. If you own a restaurant, you wouldn't want to send a coupon for a steak dinner to a vegetarian, right? Unless you're anti-herbivore, of course …

Conversion Rate

The percentage of people who completed a desired action on a single web page, such as filling out a form. Pages with high conversion rates are performing well, while pages with low conversion rates are performing poorly.

Conversion Rate Optimization (CRO)

The process of improving your site conversion using design techniques, key optimization principles, and testing. It involves creating an experience for your website visitors that will convert them into customers. CRO is most often applied to web page or landing page optimization, but it can also be applied to social media, CTAs, and other parts of your marketing.

Cost-per-Lead (CPL)

The amount it costs your marketing organization to acquire a lead. This factors heavily into CAC (customer acquisition cost), and is a metric marketers should keep a keen eye on.

D
Dynamic Content

A way to display different messaging on your website based on the information you already know about the visitor.

For example, you could use Smart CTAs so that first-time visitors will see a personalized CTA (perhaps with a top-of-the-funnel offer) and those already in your database see a different CTA (maybe for content that offers a little more information about your product or service).

E
Ebook

Ebooks are a common type of content that many marketers use, often to help generate leads. They are generally a more long-form content type than, say, blog posts, and go into in-depth detail on a subject.

Email

In its most basic sense, email stands for "Electronic Mail." It's a core component of marketing because it's a direct connection to a contact's inbox.

However, with great power comes great responsibility, meaning it's important for marketers to not abuse the email relationship with a contact. It's far too easy for a contact to click "unsubscribe" after gaining their hard earned trust in your communication. Don't blow it.

Engagement Rate

A popular social media metric used to describe the amount of interaction -- Likes, shares, comments -- a piece of content receives.

Interactions like these tell you that your messages are resonating with your fans and followers. (Click here for engagement rate benchmarks for a range of different industries.)

F
Facebook

Facebook is a social network you're likely quite familiar with already -- but it has become so much more than just a platform to publish content and gain followers.

You can now utilize the awesome targeting options available through Facebook advertising to find and attract brand new contacts to your website and get them to convert on your landing pages ... but remember, you still need awesome content to do it.

While it's a core component of any marketing strategy, it shouldn't be the only component. Focusing entirely on Facebook (or any other large social channel, for that matter) will only give you a small piece of the inbound marketing pie.

And it's still piping hot, so be careful.

G
Google+

Google+ (referred to as "Google Plus") is a social network that allows you to join and create circles in which you can mix and match family members, friends, colleagues, and fellow industry members.

While you can use it much like other social networks -- to publish and share content, and generate new leads -- it also provides content marketers with tremendous SEO value due to the rising importance of social sharing in search engine algorithms. (It is owned by Google, after all.)

H

Hashtag

Hashtags are a way for you and your readers to interact with each other on social media and have conversations about a particular piece of content.

They tie public conversations on Twitter, Facebook, and Instagram together into a single stream, which users can find by searching for a hashtag, clicking on one, or using a third-party monitoring tool like HubSpot's Social Inbox.

The hashtags themselves are simply a keyword phrase, spelled out without spaces, with a pound sign (#) in front of it -- like #InboundChat and #ChocolateLovers. You can put these hashtags anywhere in your social media posts.

I
Inbound Marketing

Inbound marketing refers to marketing activities that draw visitors in,rather than marketers having to go out to get prospects' attention. It's all about earning the attention of customers, making the company easy to find online, and drawing customers to the website by producing interesting, helpful content.

By aligning the content you publish with your customer's interests, you naturally attract inbound traffic that you can then convert, close, and delight over time.

Inbound Link

An inbound link is a link coming from another site to your own website. "Inbound" is generally used by the person receiving the link.

Websites that receive many inbound links can be more likely to rank higher in search engines. They also help folks receive referral traffic from other websites.
Infographic

A highly visual piece of content that is very popular among digital marketers as a way of relaying complex concepts in a simple and visual way.

K
Keyword

Sometimes referred to as "keyword phrases," keywords are the topics that webpages get indexed for in search results by engines like Google, Yahoo, and Bing.

Picking keywords that you'll optimize a webpage for is a two-part effort. First, you'll want to ensure the keyword has significant search volume and is not too difficult to rank for. Then, you'll want to ensure it aligns with your target audience

After deciding the appropriate keywords you want to rank for, you'll then need to optimize the appropriate pages on your website using both on-page and off-page tactics. What are those, you ask? Skip to "O" to find out -- but don't tell "L", "M", or "N"!

L
Landing Page

A landing page is a website page containing a form that is used for lead generation. This page revolves around a marketing offer, such as an ebook or a webinar, and serves to capture visitor information in exchange for the valuable offer.

Landing pages are the gatekeepers of the conversion path and are what separates a website visitor from becoming a lead.

A smart inbound marketer will create landing pages that appeal to different personae (plural for persona) at various stages of the buying process.

A hefty endeavor no doubt, but one that pays off in spades.

Lead

A person or company who's shown interest in a product or service in some way, shape, or form.

Perhaps they filled out a form, subscribed to a blog, or shared their contact information in exchange for a coupon.

Generating leads is a critical part of a prospect's journey to becoming a customer, and it falls in between the second and third stages of the larger inbound marketing methodology, which you can see below.

Lead Nurturing

Sometimes referred to as "drip marketing," lead nurturing is the practice of developing a series of communications (emails, social media messages, etc.) that seek to qualify a lead, keep it engaged, and gradually push it down the sales funnel. Inbound marketing is all about delivering valuable content to the right audience -- and lead nurturing helps foster this by providing contextually relevant information to a lead during different stages of the buying lifecycle.

M
Middle of the Funnel

This refers to the stage that a lead enters after identifying a problem. Now they're looking to conduct further research to find a solution to the problem.

Typical middle of the funnel offers include case studies or product brochures -- essentially anything that brings your business into the equation as a solution to the problem the lead is looking to solve. Also, if you want to be cool, you can refer to this stage as "MOFU" for short.

Mobile Marketing

With mobile search queries officially surpassing desktop queries, now is probably the time to explore mobile marketing.
What is it? Well, mobile marketing refers to the practice of optimizing marketing for mobile devices to provide visitors with time- and location-sensitive, personalized information for promoting goods, services, and ideas.

Mobile Optimization

Mobile optimization means designing and formatting your website so that it's easy to read and navigate from a mobile device. This can be done by either creating a separate mobile website or incorporating responsive design in initial site layout. Google's algorithm now rewards mobile-friendly websites, so if your site isn't fully optimized for mobile devices, you will likely see a hit to your ranking on mobile searches.
Monthly Recurring Revenue (MRR)

The amount of revenue a subscription-based business receives per month. Includes MRR gained by new accounts (net new), MRR gained from upsells (net positive), MRR lost from downsells (net negative), and MRR lost from cancellations (net loss).

N
Native Advertising

A type of online advertising that takes on the form and function of the platform it appears on.

Its purpose is to make ads feel less like ads, and more like part of the conversation. That means it's usually a piece of sponsored content that's relative to the consumer experience, isn't interruptive, and looks and feels similar to its editorial environment.

Native advertising can come in many forms, whether it's radio announcers talking favorably about a product sponsoring the show, or an article about a product or company showing up in your news source.

O
Offer

Offers are content assets that live behind a form on a landing page. Their primary purpose is to help marketers generate leads for your business.

There are many different types of offers you could create, including ebooks, checklists, cheat sheets, webinars, demos, templates, and tools. (If you need help putting together some high-quality offers your buyer personas will love, take some time to read over this post.)

P
Page View

A request to load a single web page on the internet. Marketers use them to analyze their website and to see if any change on the webpage results in more or fewer page views.

Pay-per-Click (PPC)

The amount of money spent to get a digital advertisement clicked. Also an internet advertising model where advertisers pay a publisher (usually a search engine, social media site, or website owner) a certain amount of money every time their ad is clicked.

For search engines, PPC ads display an advertisement when someone searches for a keyword that matches the advertiser's keyword list, which they submit to the search engine ahead of time.

PPC ads are used to direct traffic to the advertiser's website, and PPC is used to assess the cost effectiveness and profitability of your paid advertising campaigns.

There are two ways to pay for PPC ads:

Flat rate: where the advertiser and publisher agree on a fixed amount that will be paid for each click. Typically this happens when publishers have a fixed rate for PPC in different areas on their website.

Bid-based: where the advertiser competes against other advertisers in an advertising network. In this case, each advertiser sets a maximum spend to pay for a given ad spot, so the ad will stop appearing on a given website once that amount of money is spent.

It also means that the more people that click on your ad, the lower PPC you'll pay and vice versa.

Q
Qualified Lead

A contact that opted in to receive communication from your company, became educated about your product or service, and is interested in learning more.

Marketing and Sales often have two different versions of qualified leads (MQLs for Marketing, and SQLs for Sales), so be sure to have conversations with your sales team to set expectations for the types of leads you plan to hand over.

R
Responsive Design

This is the practice of developing a website that adapts accordingly to how someone is viewing it.

Instead of building a separate, distinct website for each specific device it could be viewed on, the site recognizes the device that your visitor is using and automatically generates a page that is responsive to the device the content is being viewed on -- making websites always appear optimized for screens of any dimension.

Return on Investment (ROI)

A performance measure used to evaluate the efficiency and profitability of an investment, or to compare the efficiency and profitability of multiple investments.

The formula for ROI is: (Gain from Investment minus Cost of Investment), all divided by (Cost of Investment). The result is expressed as a percentage or ratio.

If ROI is negative, then that initiative is losing the company money. The calculation can vary depending on what you input for gains and costs.

Today, marketers want to measure the ROI on every tactic and channel they use.
Many facets of marketing have pretty straightforward ROI calculations (like PPC), but others are more difficult (like content marketing).

S
Search Engine Optimization (SEO)

The practice of enhancing where a webpage appears in search results. By adjusting a webpage's on-page SEO elements and influencing off-page SEO factors, an inbound marketer can improve where a webpage appears in search engine results.

There are a ton of components to improving the SEO of your site pages. Search engines look for elements including title tags, keywords, image tags, internal link structure, and inbound links -- and that's just to name a few. Search engines also look at site structure and design, visitor behavior, and other external, off-site factors to determine how highly ranked your site should be in the search engine results pages.

Social Media

Social media is media designed to be disseminated through social interaction, created using highly accessible and scalable publishing techniques.

Facebook, Twitter, YouTube, LinkedIn and Google+ are examples of social media networks that one can join for personal or business use. Social Media is a core component of Inbound, as it provides marketers with additional channels to spread reach, increase growth, and reach business goals.

Social Proof

Social proof refers to a psychological phenomenon in which people seek direction from those around them to determine how they are supposed to act or think in a given situation. It's like when you see a really long line outside a nightclub and assume that club is really good because it's in such high demand.

In social media, social proof can be identified by the number of interactions a piece of content receives or the number of followers you have. The idea is that if others are sharing something or following someone, it must be good.

T
Top of the Funnel

Sometimes called "TOFU", top of the funnel refers to the very first stage of the buying process. Leads at this stage are just identifying a problem that they have and are looking for more information.

As such, an inbound marketer will want to create helpful content that aids leads in identifying this problem and providing next steps toward a solution. TOFU is also very tasty in certain Thai dishes.

Twitter

For the sake of creativity, I'll define Twitter in 140 characters or less: "Twitter is a platform that allows users to share 140-character long messages publicly. User can follow one another and be followed back."

U
Unique Visitor

A person who visits a website more than once within a period of time.

Marketers use this term in contrast with overall site visits to track the amount of traffic on their website. If only one person visits a webpage 30 times, then that web page has one UV and 30 total site visits.

URL

This is short for Uniform Resource Locator. I honestly didn't know that before writing this definition.

Basically, this is the address of a piece of information that can be found on the web such as a page, image, or document.

URLs are important for on-page SEO, as search engines scour the included text when mining for keywords. If a keyword you're looking to get indexed for is in the URL, you'll get brownie points from search engines (but no real brownies, unfortunately).

V
Viral Content

This term is used to describe a piece of content that has become wildly popular across the web through sharing.

Oftentimes, folks don't know a piece they're creating will be viral until it actually does, which is usually unfortunate if it's particularly embarrassing.

W
Website

A website is a set of interconnected webpages, usually including a homepage, generally located on the same server, and prepared.
And maintained as a collection of information by a person, group, or organization.

An inbound marketer should structure a website like a dynamic, multi-dimensional entity that can be used to attract relevant website visitors, convert those visitors into leads, and close those leads into customers.

Otherwise, it's just a brochure -- and let's be honest -- could you really use another brochure?

Word-of-Mouth (WOM)

The passing of information from person to person. Technically, the term refers to oral communication, but today it refers to online communication, as well.

WOM marketing is inexpensive, but it takes work and involves leveraging many components of inbound marketing like product marketing, content marketing, and social media marketing.

Workflow

A workflow is another way to describe a lead nurturing campaign. It's a set of triggers and events that move a lead through the nurturing process.

A workflow can also serve other purposes, such as adjust contact properties on a lead record based on certain conditions, or adding a contact record to a certain list.

Regardless of how you use it, workflows can be a very powerful asset in an inbound marketing strategy.

Y
YouTube

YouTube is a video-sharing website on which users can upload, share, and view videos.

Three former PayPal employees created YouTube in February 2005. In November 2006, YouTube, LLC was bought by Google Inc. for $1.65 billion, and is now operated as a subsidiary of Google. YouTube is the largest video-sharing site in the world and you're probably on it now instead of finishing up this post.

Referenced from:
https://blog.hubspot.com/marketing/inbound-marketing-glossary-list

Made in the USA
Middletown, DE
16 November 2020